The Electronic Congress

The
Electronic
Congress

A Blueprint for
Participatory Democracy

TED WACHTEL

The Piper's Press
Pipersville, Pennsylvania

10 9 8 7 6 5 4 3 2 1
First Edition

The Piper's Press
P.O. Box 400
Pipersville, PA 18947

Wachtel, Ted
The Electronic Congress:
A Blueprint for Participatory Democracy
Library of Congress Catalog Card Number: 92-64261
ISBN 0-9633887-0-3

For Susan

Contents

Prudence, indeed, will dictate that
Governments long established should not
be changed for light and transient Causes.

Declaration of Independence
1776

1

An Era of
Disillusionment

When I was 14, John F. Kennedy's presidential campaign came to town. Students got the day off from school so I went downtown to see his motorcade. I watched from a window in the old YMCA building, several stories above the platform on Monument Square as Kennedy gave his speech. His vigor and enthusiasm excited me. Months later I recorded the words of his inaugural address from television with a big black Webcor reel-to-reel tape recorder and played his speech over and over:

"The energy, the faith, the devotion which we bring to this endeavor will light our country and all who serve it, and the glow from that fire can truly light the world. And so, my fellow Americans, ask not what your country can do for you, ask what you can do for your country."

Kennedy made me feel that I had the power to change things and that I was responsible for more than just myself. I had a responsibility to my country and to the world as well. I felt confident that I would find a role to play and I was anxious for the chance to get involved. I fantasized about joining the Peace Corps and helping poor people in other countries, or joining the military and fighting communism, or becoming president some day and making the world a better place.

My political consciousness awakened during the Kennedy presidency. He and his brother, Robert Kennedy, inspired me. I believed in my country and its institutions. While I knew we were not perfect, I was confident that America was the best country in the world and would keep getting better. I assumed that the president, Congress and other leaders had my best interests at heart and were all capable and truthful people. Although I had never voted, I felt connected to my government and its leaders and believed that my government belonged to me.

When Kennedy was shot in Dallas, my view of reality began to crumble. For my generation, the assassination was a watershed from which coursed an era of conflict and upheaval. During that era I learned to doubt my government.

I went to college in the fall after Kennedy's death, intending to become a politician. I majored in government but eventually changed to history when I decided I might better serve the public as a teacher.

The Vietnam War intensified, making soldiers of young men all around me. Although I still believed that my leaders were telling me the truth, two things shook my trust. First, a friend's brother, David, was killed in Vietnam. I went to the funeral where the minister read from his letters. David, who had volunteered for military service, said that he felt like a Nazi soldier as he burned the homes of innocent people. His view of the war clashed sharply with what my leaders were telling me. Second, as part of my studies I did an extensive research paper on the origins of the Vietnam conflict. What I learned through my reading contradicted what my leaders were saying.

From enemy casualty counts to unfulfilled predictions of military victory, my country's leaders squandered their credibility on a daily basis. President Lyndon Johnson gave way to President Richard Nixon, whose proposal to turn the fighting over to the Vietnamese led to the final debacle of the fall of Saigon. The truth—that we Americans completely misunderstood the Vietnamese people—revealed itself.

The late '60s and early '70s were filled with events that shook my faith: the assassinations of Martin Luther King and Robert Kennedy, the police riot at the Chicago Democratic convention, the killings of students at Kent State and Jackson State, the revelations of our military's deceit in the "Pentagon Papers." Although I never agreed with the strident criticisms of the radicals who compared

America to Nazi Germany, I felt betrayed by my
leaders' lack of candor and responsiveness to the
legitimate concerns and rights of citizens in a democratic society. I was also dismayed by the passivity
of many fellow Americans who felt that we had no
right to question authority, that being a good citizen
demanded an unquestioning loyalty to our government and its leaders.

Both my wife Susan and I became teachers in a
rural community. In 1972 we volunteered for the
McGovern campaign in hopes of ending the Vietnam
War. Inspired by McGovern's morality, we were
disappointed by his ineffectual campaign. Still, we
won a write-in vote to become our precinct's representatives to the county Democratic Party committee
and hoped to make a contribution through political
involvement.

At party meetings county leaders were backed
by the votes of political hacks with government jobs.
Real democratic decision-making was not practiced.
We found it impossible to advise our friends and
neighbors to vote for those of our party's candidates
whose opponents were clearly superior choices. Disappointed by our experience, we eventually let our
formal relationship with the party lapse.

In the summer of the McGovern campaign, a
burglary at the headquarters of the Democratic
National Committee in the Watergate office building began the two-year saga which resulted in
President Nixon's resignation. Although I was
upset by the abuses of power which the Watergate

investigation revealed, I was most disturbed by the unwillingness of so many people to believe the unpleasant truth as it was exposed in the Congressional hearings.

In the midst of the hearings a woman who worked at my school angrily confronted me about my view of the situation, which she described as disloyalty to the president. To her I represented all the protesters who had challenged the Vietnam War and American values and now were tearing down the presidency. At the time I was upset by her denial of the facts, but I only had to remember my early faith in government and its undoing to understand the pain she was feeling. Our schools, our media and our culture had taught us to see a government without blemishes, a very comforting image. Giving that up for a more disturbing view, showing the warts and scars of our political system and its leadership, was extremely difficult.

The vote for impeachment by the committee members of the House of Representatives convinced all but the most die-hard Nixon supporters that the President was lying, that he had abused his power and had participated in a cover-up of the misdeeds of his staff. A short time after Nixon resigned the same woman came to me and apologized. She admitted that she had been unwilling to accept what had now become an undeniable truth. I thanked her for her apology.

After Watergate I hoped that government would get better, that it would reform and begin to address

many of the issues which concerned me, that it
would be more responsive to its citizens. Instead,
our national government became even more responsive to special interest groups. One scandal after
another revealed how corrupt our national government was: Abscam, Iran-Contra, the savings and
loan bailout, the BCCI scandal, the Keating Five. I
felt overwhelmed in the '80s as my government
seemed to drift further and further away from me:
huge deficits and burgeoning national debt, restruc-
turing of income taxes to benefit the wealthy, hollow
promises of environmental and educational reform,
insensitivity to the needs of the poor and the home-
less.

Worst of all, I felt powerless to do anything about
it. Having abandoned our direct political involvement in party politics because we felt our efforts
were wasted, Susan and I occasionally campaigned
for candidates from either party whom we admired.
We maintained our membership in Common Cause,
a national bipartisan citizens' lobby for good government, and other state and national organizations
which support legislative activity consistent with
our personal views. We voted regularly and we
wrote letters or made telephone calls to our state
and federal legislators whenever we felt we could
help support a particular piece of legislation.

In our personal lives we now had children. I left
my position as history teacher to become the school
district's media coordinator and initiated a public
cable channel, which provided television coverage of

school board meetings and politics on a local level. Eventually, I left public schools, and Susan and I established the Community Service Foundation, a non-profit agency which provides education, counseling and residential services for troubled adolescents. Through the Foundation's work I became one of the founders of the national TOUGHLOVE movement, which organized support groups for parents of troubled teenagers, and I co-authored several TOUGHLOVE books. I still felt ineffectual as a citizen of the American republic, however, and I wanted to do something about it.

I had come to realize that supporting candidates was not an effective way to support the enactment of a specific law on a specific issue. Even contacting legislators seemed of questionable value. While my legislators often shared my views, I did not trust that they would respond to my entreaties or those of my fellow citizens as much as they would to those coming from people or organizations who gave large sums of money to their campaigns.

The National Rifle Association provides an obvious example of a well-financed and powerful group influencing policy despite contrary popular sentiment. Its political action committee, the fifth most generous in the country, spent nearly $4.7 million to back political candidates in the 1988 election. The NRA opposes all gun-control legislation, although 87 percent of American gun owners, according to a 1989 Time/CNN Poll, favor "a federal law requiring a seven-day waiting period and a background check

for anyone who wants to buy a handgun."[1] Despite
the active support of Sarah Brady and her husband
Jim, who was shot and paralyzed in John Hinckley's
assassination attempt on President Ronald Reagan,
the "Brady bill" still languishes in the Senate in
mid-1992. Our representative government seems to
have difficulty translating the will of its citizens into
law.

Gun-control legislation is not an isolated example of public policy failing to coincide with public
opinion. A 1978 Gallup poll assessed public opinion
on 14 national issues and found that public policy
contradicted public opinion more often than it con-
curred. The poll determined that on only six of the
14 issues did our national government abide by its
citizens' views.[2]

The frustration caused by my inability to directly affect important national issues led me to
propose the Electronic Congress, a nationwide referendum system through which citizens can join
legislators in affecting issues and deciding laws.

I began working on this book in 1990. I assumed
that I would have to make an elaborate case to show
how badly our representative government was working. I believed that I would have to muster all kinds
of evidence to persuade my fellow Americans that
we need a change in our national government. I
invited my son Joshua, a history major at Penn
State University with an interest in government, to
assist me with research and editing. As we worked
on the book in 1992, events occurred which made it

obvious that a vast number of Americans already believed that our representative government was in serious trouble.

The most dramatic indication that Americans felt betrayed by their elected representatives and government was the phenomenon of Ross Perot. An independent candidate for the American presidency, he upstaged both incumbent Republican President George Bush and Democratic challenger Bill Clinton by leading both party candidates in election polls in the spring of 1992. Although he won no electoral votes, Perot's 19 percent share of the popular vote in the presidential election demonstrated the public's discontent with our current political system.

Another indication of trouble was the decision of 56 members of Congress not to seek re-election in 1992, the largest voluntary departure since World War I. Representative Vin Weber (R-Minnesota), one of the 56, participating in a mid-1992 round-table discussion about the defection, said:

"We are in a decaying spiral of public confidence. The public does not trust the institutions; they don't trust the political parties. It used to be, 'I hate the Congress, but I love my Congressman.' Now they've decided they hate their Congressman, too."[3]

The abrupt retirement of so many legislators was in part due to another of the many scandals which have undermined our faith in our elected representatives in recent years: the revelation that 355 members of the House of Representatives had collectively bounced more than 20,000 checks worth almost $11 million over a three-year period at the House bank.[4] Some of the worst offenders decided not to run for office because they knew they would be defeated for abusing their bank privileges, but reputable legislators also left because of their own disillusionment with our government.

Senator Warren Rudman (R-New Hampshire), one of our most respected national legislators, was among those who decided to retire. "I am very frustrated with the inability of Congress to accomplish a great deal. Congress is not facing the fundamental issues," he said in an interview. "The one I've talked about the most is the deficit...which will truly wreck the country .... We ought to tell [people] what the real facts are. We ought to do what we have to do, go home and try to defend it. The worst thing that can happen to a politician is to get defeated .... And frankly I'm not sure the power is worth holding on to if what we're doing is bankrupting America."[5]

Cynicism toward government grows steadily while the number of people who vote in elections dwindles. In the late 1800s voter participation was between 70 and 80 percent, but for most of this century we have rarely exceeded 60 percent. In the last 30 years we have experienced a substantial decrease in voting without any sign of rebounding. Half of Americans eligible to vote are staying away in presidential elections and two-thirds fail to vote in off-year congressional elections.[6]

The reason that people fail to vote is that they see

no connection between voting and results. African-American voters represent a major exception to this pattern. Since the advent of civil rights legislation and voter registration campaigns, African-American voters have seen their participation in elections produce a significant increase in the number of African-American elected officials, most notably among big city mayors. This connection between voting and observable results has encouraged African-American voters, but other voters have increasingly turned away from the polls.[7]

We know that our elected leaders are supposed to serve the general welfare of all Americans but we see that Congress generally responds to the demands of special interest groups. Two-thirds of Americans are convinced that government is dominated by a few big interests looking out for only themselves.[8]

"Congress is awash in money. Interests have emerged that have enormous amounts of cash and that stand between the Congress and its constituency," said Senator Tim Worth (D-Colorado), also voluntarily retiring. "In my 18 years in Congress I have seen the denominator of debate get lower and lower, and I think much of that is explained by fear—fear that you will be unable to raise money from a certain group; or worse that the interest group will give the money to the other guy. . . ."[9]

Our legislators need our help. The worst of them have sold us out and the best cannot save the republic by themselves. We need a mechanism to connect us with them, especially when the pressure from special interests works against the common good. I propose the Electronic Congress as that mechanism. It would connect us to our government and our leaders so that we can feel, once again, that our government belongs to us.

2

Citizen Lawmakers

The Electronic Congress would be a national
referendum system whose primary function would
be to help restore public confidence in representative government. It would create a partnership
between Americans and their congressmen and a
new role for voters in federal government as citizen
lawmakers.

While almost all states employ referendum and
other forms of direct democracy to involve citizens in
law-making, this nation does not. Referendum is
the most common form of direct democracy whereby
issues are placed on the ballot by legislatures, county
and municipal councils or school boards for direct
approval or disapproval by voters. Americans could
participate in the national legislative decision-

making process by voting in monthly or quarterly telephone referendums on two types of ballot questions—binding or advisory. On binding questions, citizens would vote yes or no to enact or defeat specific resolutions proposed by Congress. The outcome would be binding, as if the votes had been cast by senators and representatives themselves. On the other type, multiple-choice or yes-or-no advisory questions, the result would not be binding. Legislators could consider voter preferences as indicated by responses to advisory questions when deciding legislation on the same topics at a later date.

Rather than wait for regular primary or general elections in the spring and fall of each year, referendums could be scheduled at any time. Votes would be cast by telephone, using Touch-Tone signals to indicate preferences on each ballot question. Voters would call free 800-numbers. Although the idea of voting by telephone may seem novel, the technology is well-established.

The idea of telephone voting for candidates or for referendum questions has been advocated by many, including Ross Perot, who called for "electronic town meetings;"[1] Evan Ravitz, executive director of the Colorado-based Voting by Phone Foundation, who advocates telephone voting in regular elections,[2] and the innovative Buckminster Fuller, who first proposed telephone voting on Congressional questions more than 50 years ago.[3]

The Electronic Congress concept would not only

be a telephone voting system, but also would integrate existing media and technology with the traditional legislative activities of congressmen. What makes the Electronic Congress "electronic" would be its use of the country's electronic communications network to include all citizens in the Congressional decision-making process.

A Vast Electronic Congress

In the Electronic Congress Americans would vote on issues which congressmen select for public participation. Over a period of a month or more people would hear legislators and others debate these issues on radio and television, voice opinions on call-in shows, read about upcoming choices in newspapers and magazines, debate the issues in workplaces and communities and read and write letters to the editors of publications. On the appointed days, they would review voting guides, pick up telephones and vote. When the referendum voting ended, computers would tally the results for dissemination by national media.

On binding ballot questions, voters would assume the roles of legislators. Hearing and viewing Congressional debates through national broadcast media and voting to enact or defeat bills through the national telephone network, citizens would constitute a vast Electronic Congress.

Citizens' colleagues in that Electronic Congress, U.S. senators and representatives, would choose and frame the questions on the ballot. Although most bills would be decided by the two houses of Congress through the traditional legislative process, either House or Senate could designate controversial or important bills to be presented to the citizens for a yes-or-no vote. The Electronic Congress would not decide issues by national popular majority. The majority vote would be determined in each Congressional district and in each state. With each district casting one vote in the House and each state casting two votes in the Senate, the final outcome would be decided by separate votes in the House and the Senate. If there were a tie in the Senate, the vice-president could vote to break the tie, as the Constitution presently provides. A resolution would have to pass both House and Senate to go on to the president for consideration.

The creation of a bicameral legislature, with a House and a Senate, was an important compromise which resolved the competing interests of large and small states at the Constitutional Convention. The Electronic Congress concept preserves that compromise because less populous states retain the equality they have always had with larger states in the Senate. Wyoming and California have the same two votes. In the House of Representatives, more populous states with more Congressional districts still have proportionately more representation.

The Electronic Congress would also preserve the right of the president to veto legislation after the outcome is determined by the House and Senate. The citizenry could override the president's veto in a subsequent vote, assuming that more than two-thirds of the districts and states were to vote against the president's action. Thus, the Electronic Congress would maintain the traditional checks and balances incorporated in the Constitution at its inception, while increasing citizen involvement in government.

A Constitutional Amendment

Congress could implement an Electronic Congress without any change in the Constitution if referendums were limited to advisory questions. To transfer some of its authority to the voting public through binding questions, however, Congress would have to propose a Constitutional amendment.

*AN AMENDMENT
TO THE CONSTITUTION OF
THE UNITED STATES OF AMERICA*

ARTICLE

Section 1. The Congress shall have the right to delegate its legislative function on a bill, by a majority vote in either the House of Representatives or the Senate, to a referendum by the voters of the United States. The House may not delegate its sole power to impeach and the Senate may not delegate its power to consent to treaties or appointments nor its sole power to try all impeachments.

Section 2. The referendum vote on each bill shall be tallied by Congressional district and by State. One yea or nay vote shall be cast in the House of Representatives to reflect the majority vote in each respective Congressional district. Two yea or nay votes shall be cast in the Senate to reflect the majority vote in each respective State. If the Senate vote is equally divided, the Vice President shall have a vote.

Section 3. Any bill receiving a majority of votes in both the House of Representatives and the Senate in a referendum shall be presented to the President, the same as a bill passed by Congress. If the President returns the bill, with his objections, to Congress, the bill shall be subject to a second referendum. If approved by two-thirds of both Houses, it shall become law.

Section 4. The Congress shall establish the procedures for referendum by the voters.

This amendment, like any other Constitutional amendment, must be ratified by 38 state legislatures (or state conventions).

Other Levels of Government

The Electronic Congress concept has important implications for states, counties, municipal governments and school districts. Whether government referendums employ binding or advisory questions, the techniques of the Electronic Congress can be helpful to any level of government. Whenever leaders must ascertain public opinion on a given issue, a telephone referendum system could be a timely and cost-effective way to measure it. A school board, for example, could base budget decisions on a precise assessment of the public's stated priorities, rather than judging its mood from letters to the editor, angry speakers at meetings or other informal communications, which may not be the majority view.

States, particularly those states which have held referendums for decades, may be particularly receptive to the idea of an "electronic legislature." The referendum process would be separate from candidate elections, allowing citizens to focus only on ballot questions when they voted. Referendums could also be held more frequently and issues could be addressed in a more timely fashion than twice yearly elections now afford.

Initiative Questions and Electronic Petitioning

As an additional component of the Electronic Congress, citizens themselves may want to initiate questions for the referendum ballot. By getting a required number of signatures on petitions, anyone could propose a ballot question and have it offered to the public for consideration. This process of "popular initiative" would further enhance the opportunity for public participation in national affairs.

The Electronic Congress would allow only advisory votes on ballot questions proposed by popular initiative, rather than binding votes. Permitting binding votes on initiatives would require further Constitutional amendment, an unlikely prospect because some of the 28 state legislatures which do not allow their citizens to propose and vote on initiative questions would have to vote for ratification.

Getting signatures from a large number of people would be difficult and costly. To expedite the process, a smaller number of signatures could be required in the initial phase of the petition process, perhaps tens of thousands from a minimum number of states. The petitioning process itself could then move into an electronic phase whereby the proposed question would be announced and placed on the Electronic Congress computer system. Registered voters could call in and electronically enlist as supporters of the petition drive. After enlisting several million supporters for its electronic petition, the question would be placed on an upcoming ballot of the Electronic Congress.

The electronic petitioning process would simplify the existing procedure, reducing the cost of initiating a ballot question for both citizens and government. The task of verifying valid signatures would be eliminated because only registered voters could enlist by telephone as supporters of an initiative.

Why Not Polls Instead?

Polls, an established means of assessing public opinion, are costly. They also lack precision. Because pollsters sample only a portion of the public, there is always a margin of error. Even if pollsters contact only registered voters, they can neither be certain that people will actually bother to vote, nor that people are telling the truth about how they will vote. Polls are not credible enough to speak conclusively for the voting public, particularly on controversial issues. The telephone referendum system, on the other hand, counts the votes of all the voters. The results are, by definition, an exact measure of the voting public's views at a given time.

Conclusion

Telephone voting in national referendums would provide increased opportunity for citizens to communicate with their congressmen and to participate directly in decision-making. The frequent use of referendums with either advisory or binding questions would represent a dramatic change in the way the national government does business. Yet, the American republic has often changed. Over the last 200 years, eligibility for participation in our representative form of government has evolved from a very narrow group of voters, white males with property, to a much more inclusive constituency. The Electronic Congress, which gives citizens a new role as lawmakers, would be another important step in the evolution toward a more democratic American government.

3

An Evolving Democracy

The Americans who wrote the Constitution in 1787 had no intention of creating a democracy. They were leery of entrusting too many people with too much power. They were aware of the failings of past democracies, such as Athens, Rome and Venice, which had not sustained themselves. While inspired by the democratic ideals of philosophers, such as Montesquieu and Rousseau, who believed that the people should have the sole power to author and enact the laws, the framers of the Constitution were not willing to trust the masses completely.

Creating a Republic

James Madison, advocating for the Constitution

in a series of essays called *The Federalist Papers*, distinguished between a Republic, in which citizens elect representatives to legislate for them, and a Democracy, in which all citizens serve as legislators. Madison and his peers at the Constitutional Convention hoped to establish a representative government that was better than pure democracy and which did not suffer "the mortal diseases under which popular governments have every where perished." [1]

They had a healthy skepticism about human nature and tried to establish checks and balances against the abuse of power by any branch of government. The bicameral Congress not only represented a compromise between the smallest and largest states, but also appeased those who feared the potential abuses of a popularly elected House of Representatives. The Senate, whose members were selected by state legislatures rather than the public, offset the power of the House.

The Constitution also distanced the citizenry from actual selection of the president by establishing an Electoral College. State legislatures or the voters in each state selected representatives to the Electoral College, who in turn elected the president and vice-president. That system persists today, a clear reminder of our founding fathers' reluctance to trust us with too much power.

Madison feared that a faction, when finding itself in the majority, might serve only its own interests and too easily trample the rights of a minority or the general well-being of the nation. He believed that the effect of a representative system would be "to refine and enlarge the public views, by passing them through the medium of a chosen body of citizens . . . ."[2]

The authors of the Constitution came from America's wealthiest classes and were viewed with suspicion by the more radical leaders of the Revolutionary era, such as Patrick Henry, who believed that the number of representatives comprising the proposed government was too small. He ridiculed Madison's argument that a representative system would "refine" the public views. "If, sir, the diminution of numbers be an augmentation of merit, perfection must center in one . . . . If ten men be better than one hundred and seventy, it follows of necessity that one is better than ten—the choice is more refined."[3]

Madison felt that a balance must be struck. The number of voters represented by each legislator should be numerous enough to prevent local interests from being forced on the representative, but few enough to keep local interests from being engulfed by national interests.[4] He feared that too many legislators in Congress, no matter how qualified, would foster "confusion and intemperance." He wrote, "Had every Athenian citizen been a Socrates; every Athenian assembly would still have been a mob."[5]

Madison and his peers were concerned that a large, popularly elected assembly might turn into a

mob. The framers of the Constitution were affluent
men, and their caution was partially based on their
concern that a propertyless rabble might seize their
wealth. As Madison put it, "Those who hold, and
those who are without property, have ever formed
distinct interests in society."[6]

Although most of the founders of our republic
had a deep regard for the rights of the "common
man" they wondered whether common men could
successfully run a government. They limited the
number of representatives in the Senate to two from
each state. They saw the greatest potential for mob
behavior in the House, where the representatives
would be elected by the people themselves. The
framers of the Constitution limited the number of
legislators in the House of Representatives by requiring that the "number of Representatives shall
not exceed one for every thirty thousand . . . ."

Besides limiting the number of representatives
in the popularly elected House and distancing the
selection of senators and the president from the
people, the founders could also assume that those
who were allowed to vote would be very much like
them, white males who owned property. Had the
American government failed to change, it would be
a very different nation today.

Making Changes

We began to modify our Constitution almost
immediately when 10 amendments, the Bill of Rights,

were added to the Constitution in the first session of
Congress in 1789. These amendments insured individual liberties and limited the powers of the federal
government. They were ratified in 1791 and established a precedent for making changes.

   The wealthy, aristocratic interests which dominated the Constitutional Convention were soon
overturned by the election of Thomas Jefferson in
1800. Though of the propertied class themselves,
both Jefferson and another popular president in the
1830s, Andrew Jackson, built their political careers
on the support of the "common man." Their efforts
contributed to important changes in the criteria for
voting, especially the reduction and eventual aboli-
tion of property requirements which, in most states,
was completed by the middle of the century. As
more voting restrictions fell in the subsequent decades and less affluent Americans attained the
right to vote, the fears of the wealthy, that the
republic would falter when suffrage was expanded,
proved unjustified. The nation was evolving toward
greater democracy.

   Further growth in suffrage was implemented
after the Civil War when slavery was abolished and
the Fifteenth Amendment, ratified in 1870, gave
African-Americans the right to vote in all states. In
1920 the Nineteenth Amendment enfranchised
women. Most recently, in 1971, the Twenty-sixth
Amendment lowered the voting age to 18.

   The Progressive Era, two decades at the turn of
the century, brought significant movement toward

more direct control by citizens over their government, another sign of an evolving democracy. The Seventeenth Amendment, ratified in 1913, provided for the direct election of senators by voters rather than by state legislatures, undoing the limitations established by the Constitutional Convention more than a century before. Many states and localities also implemented initiative, referendum and recall as a response to corrupt state legislatures. Initiative and referendum involved citizens directly in making laws, while recall allowed voters to remove public officials without waiting for their terms of office to expire.

Initiative and Referendum

In 1898 South Dakota became the first state to adopt a constitutional amendment providing for statewide initiative and referendum. Although Oregon did not do so until 1899, it was the first state to use the initiative and referendum process when its citizens approved two initiatives in 1904. In 1906 Oregonians approved three laws and four constitutional amendments among 10 initiatives placed on the ballot.[7]

Oregon's experience inspired reformers in other states. Montana passed an initiative and referendum that same year. In 1907 Oklahoma became the first state to join the Union with initiative and referendum as part of its original constitution. In the decade between 1908 and 1918 many cities and

20 additional states adopted these tools of direct democracy.[8]

No state below the Mason-Dixon line and few east of the Mississippi adopted initiative and referendum during these years. The fear of the potential power of immigrants in eastern states and of African-Americans in southern states obstructed the implementation of direct democracy on a state level in those parts of the nation.[9]

World War I brought the Progressive Era to an end, as well as the growth of statewide initiative and referendum. Not until Alaska entered the Union in 1959 did another state give its citizens the right to propose and enact their own laws. Beginning in the 1960s additional states voted to adopt initiative and referendum: Wyoming and Florida in 1968, Illinois in 1970 and the District of Columbia in 1977. In 1980 Minnesota failed to adopt initiative and referendum because voters in the general election who abstained on the question were counted as voting against the measure. Rhode Island narrowly defeated adoption in 1986.

The Progressive Era failed to achieve initiative and referendum in national government. But from 1914 to 1940 there was an effort to amend the Constitution so that the United States could not go to war without the approval of its citizens in a national referendum unless the nation was attacked or invaded. Best known by the name of its sponsor during the '30s, Representative Louis Ludlow (D-Indiana), the bill failed by only 21 votes in a test vote

in the House of Representatives in 1938. World War
II eliminated further discussion of the Ludlow
amendment. That was the closest the United States
has come to adopting a procedure for national referendum.[10]

In 1977 the Senate held hearings to consider a
Constitutional amendment allowing direct initiative on a national basis. The voter initiative process
would have allowed citizens to make a law by sub-
jecting a resolution to a national referendum after
obtaining enough valid signatures on petitions.
About three million signatures, at least three percent of registered voters, would have been required
for voters to propose a law for a national referendum. If approved by a majority vote of the citizenry,
the resolution would have bypassed the Congress
and the President and become the law of the land.

The chief proponent of this measure was James
Abourezk of South Dakota, who was about to retire
from the Senate. Two similar resolutions were
proposed concurrently in the House of Representatives. Hearings were held in the Senate
Subcommittee on the Constitution for two days,
December 13-14, 1977. Ralph Nader, the consumer
advocate, was the most well-known proponent of
direct democracy who spoke at the hearings. Most
of the others who testified—political scientists, politicians, activists and interested citizens—supported
various forms of national voter initiative.[11]

Despite a Gallup poll in May 1978, which indicated that 57 percent of the American public favored

a national initiative process, the proposed amendment never reached the Senate floor.[12] The bill was reintroduced in 1979 by 55 co-sponsors including Senators Hatfield (R-Oregon), DeConcini (D-Arizona), Simpson (R-Wyoming), Gravel (D-Alaska), Pressler (R-South Dakota), and Representatives Jones (D-Oklahoma) and Goldwater (R-Arizona). Despite support from members of both political parties, the bill failed to move in either the Senate or the House.[13]

Another co-sponsor of the 1979 national initiative legislation was Representative Jack Kemp (R-New York), a Republican presidential candidate and later President George Bush's Secretary of Housing and Urban Development. In his 1981 book, *An American Renaissance*, Kemp argued for the national initiative amendment to the Constitution: "I feel as strongly as I do about this reform because I believe it goes to the heart of our national malaise." Kemp believed that this instrument of direct democracy had the potential to reduce the alienation and distrust toward our national government found among many citizens.[14]

Other Proposals for Citizen Involvement

In the early 1960s, Representative Charles Gubser (R-California) proposed a "nationwide advisory opinion poll." The president and the minority and majority leaders of the Senate and the House would each select two questions, a total of 10, to be

asked of the American public annually by the Bu-
reau of Census. The idea received little attention or
political support.[15]

In 1980 Representative Richard A. Gephardt (D-
Missouri) proposed a national advisory referendum.
He said, "There is a growing feeling among the
American people that their votes no longer count,
that politicians fail to respond to legitimate concerns, and that they have little or no impact on
policy decisions. People are frustrated . . . . A
National Referendum will provide the vehicle for
the re-expression of public sentiment for or against
critical issues facing the Nation." His proposal
provided for up to three questions on the ballot every
two years, selected after public hearings and accompanied by a voter's guide for distribution to the
public. Although Gephardt's idea was not supported by Congress, a 1987 Gallup poll found that 58
percent of the public favored a national advisory
referendum.[16]

In 1992 the political status quo was challenged
by the unexpected presidential candidacy of wealthy
Texas businessman, Ross Perot, who proposed electronic town meetings in which political leaders
would debate issues on television followed by citizens indicating their preferences by telephone voting.

Perot described the electronic town hall with
advisory voting as his primary means for governing
as president. He claimed, "If we ever put the people
back in charge of this country and make sure they
understand the issues, you'll see the White House

and Congress, like a ballet, pirouetting around the stage getting it done in unison." On two occasions, however, he prescribed a formal, binding role for electronic town meetings when he proposed a Constitutional amendment which would transfer the authority to levy taxes from Congress to the voters.[17] By finishing such a strong third in the presidential election, Ross Perot demonstrated that he and his ideas were being taken very seriously by a great many Americans.

Outgrowing Our Representation

American government is facing a crisis of confidence among its constituents. Part of the problem is that we have outgrown our original system of representation. The framers of the Constitution limited the number of representatives in the House to no more than one for every 30,000 citizens. As of the 1990 census the average representative has more than 570,000 constituents. Two hundred years before, in 1790, Virginia, the largest state, had 747,610 people represented by two senators. Now California, the largest state, has 30 million people represented by two senators. California's present population is eight times that of the whole United States in 1790.

Each congressman in 1790 actually represented many fewer voters than the numbers indicate because all women and most African-Americans, immigrants and white males without property were

denied the right to vote in 1790. In some states there
were even religious limitations.

After each census we gain millions more people,
yet the number of federal legislators remains constant. Over a quarter-billion citizens are represented
by a mere 535 legislators. Patrick Henry's fears of
under-representation now seem justified, while
James Madison's arguments for striking a balance
between local and national interests have been
rendered obsolete.

As representation decreases in relation to our
population, the role of the individual citizen in
representative government shrinks as well. So
many compete for the attention of each senator and
representative that it is rare to have personal contact. We perceive congressmen as media celebrities,
not as people who might hear our personal views.

We can write or telephone elected officials, but
we usually receive only a computer-generated form
letter in response. We can help campaign or make
campaign contributions but our candidate, if elected,
may not vote on issues in accordance with our views.
There is no direct way for us to make our opinions on
any given national issue actually count.

The means of campaigning for election have
become less personal as well. The sheer number of
voters who comprise the constituency of each senator and representative makes it necessary for
candidates to reach people through television and
mass mailings. Old-fashioned face-to-face campaigning has been replaced by strategic appearances

where television cameras record "sound bites," short quotable remarks which fit the time constraints of the evening news. A candidate stands outside the factory entrance or shakes hands in a crowd primarily for the purpose of being videotaped for television.

The cost of purchasing television time and other media has dictated dramatic increases in campaign spending. The need for a great deal of campaign money makes candidates for public office increasingly dependent on the donations of special interest groups. Political action committees, wealthy individuals and powerful corporations donate money to campaigns in exchange for favors from government. These favors come in the form of special laws, special funding and special tax breaks. In practice our legislators are not representing us; rather, they are selling their votes to the highest bidders.

The Dominance of Special Interests

Special interest groups, such as political action committees (PACs), are what James Madison and the other members of the Constitutional Convention feared most. They foresaw the kinds of inequities which characterize today's political system and realized that legislative tasks, such as establishing taxes, required "the most exact impartiality." Such tasks would be open to great temptation for "a predominant party, to trample on the rules of justice." Such factions would not hesitate to overburden others because whatever they could get others to pay would be "a shilling saved to their own pockets." [18]

Avoiding the dominance of factions was a primary goal of the Constitutional Convention. Madison wrote: "To secure the public good, and private rights, against the danger of such a faction, and at the same time to preserve the spirit and the form of popular government is the great object to which our enquiries are directed." [19]

While James Madison feared majority factions, the greatest threat to the republic actually comes from minority factions. Tightly organized, well-financed PACs representing minority interests undermine the integrity of elected representatives. Despite the founders' best efforts, in recent years the Constitution has failed miserably in limiting the power of special interest groups. Since 1974 the number of PACs registered with the Federal Election Commission has mushroomed from 608 to over 4,000 today. [20] Since 1979 contributions from PACs nearly tripled, exceeding a third of a billion dollars in the 1988 elections. [21]

According to Common Cause, a national bipartisan citizens' group, PACs are undermining our representative system. Nationally syndicated columnist David Broder wrote in 1989, "The whole congressional environment is distorted and corrupted by the rush of money into the rigid and uncompetitive political system." Historian Henry Steele Commager has said, "Politics responds more to money and money pressures than ever before. It corrupts our society." [22]

Because politicians need so much money to get re-elected, they focus on pleasing special interests more than on representing their own constituents. Common Cause wants to remedy this by passage of comprehensive campaign-finance reform legislation which would limit campaign spending, reduce the role of special interest political money, provide alternative campaign funds and close the loopholes which allow donors to bypass federal limitations on campaign donations. These proposals can be enacted if enough Americans recognize their importance.

The Electronic Congress could further reduce the influence of special interests by allowing legislators to pass on some important decisions to their constituents. When a measure is particularly controversial and pressure from special interests is intense, congressmen might cite the controversy as justification for passing the measure to the voters to decide. For example, federal deficit reduction will require decreases in military spending, entitlements such as Social Security and other politically sensitive programs. Voters are better situated to make these difficult decisions than legislators, whose hopes for re-election are threatened by PACs opposing such cutbacks.

For many years PACs have kept Congress and the president from achieving a balanced budget. We can bemoan their lack of courage, but I suspect that many of us would act as they do if we were in their shoes. I propose that citizens shoulder the respon-

sibility. When we vote against special interest
groups in a referendum, we cannot be voted out of
office. We are not speaking for the people; we are the
people.

Citizen Involvement through Electronic Media

When the Constitution was written, direct public involvement in the legislature would have been
impractical, if not impossible. Transportation and
communication were limited to foot, horse and boat
so that information moved very slowly. Many rural
areas of the nation lacked newspapers. But technology in the 20th century has linked all the citizens of
our nation. Even the most remote communities are
connected to a national video network by cable
television and satellite transmission. In this country 93 percent of households have telephone service
and 98 percent have televisions.[23] Most of the
remainder have access to telephones and televisions. We now have a communication system so
sophisticated that each of us can instantaneously
and simultaneously witness the same event.

One of James Madison's primary arguments for
a republican form of government was that a "greater
number of citizens and extent of territory may be
brought within the compass . . . Extend the sphere,
and you take in a greater variety of parties and
interest; you make it less probable that a majority of
the whole will have a common motive to invade the
rights of other citizens."[24] Technology converts his

words into a compelling argument for including everyone in the legislative process now that it is feasible to do so. The current communication network allows our democracy to encompass more citizens and territory than Madison ever imagined.

Today, through television, hundreds of millions of observers spread over the entire nation fit into one legislative committee room. Millions of us watched Sam Ervin, John Dean and others participate in the Watergate hearings. We watched Oliver North explain his role in providing arms to Iran and the Contras. We watched Anita Hill and Clarence Thomas testify before the Senate Judiciary Committee. Millions of Americans have seen presidential candidate's television debates, beginning with Richard Nixon and John F. Kennedy. We were all there together at the same time, as if we were at a town meeting.

Technology has changed the parameters and possibilities for citizen participation. Now we can not only watch television passively as a one-way experience but also participate in a two-way experience. Americans often vote in informal polls by calling a 900-telephone number and paying a small fee to record their choices, sometimes for their favorite song on a radio station or their choice of classic football plays rebroadcast during half-time of a Monday night football game. Why couldn't these casual polls be used for more serious purposes?

Despite the instantaneous capabilities of electronic media, there are reasons the Electronic Congress would not permit immediate responses to issues raised. If as few as three percent of us used our telephones simultaneously, we would shut down the national phone system.[25] More importantly, instant referendums would be unacceptable because voters need time to make sound decisions. If we are unwilling to base referendums on emotional and superficial understandings, then we must allow at least a month to exchange views with others and digest feelings and information before reaching a conclusion.

We are just beginning to explore the possibilities of being linked electronically. We can use our technology to foster the development of a more representative system of government and, by merging referendums with broadcast media and telephone voting, we can help our democracy evolve to meet existing and future challenges.

Conclusion

The creation of an Electronic Congress would be a substantial undertaking. If any ballot question is to be more than advisory, there must be a Constitutional amendment to provide that the measure would have the force of law. Establishing an Electronic Congress would be as tenable as any other step taken in the democratic evolution of our republic. When the voting age was lowered to 18 by a Constitutional amendment in 1971, naysayers

warned of dire consequences, including the fear that
young voters would elect a rock star as president.
Every change has been opposed by those who feared
the growing democratization of political power: en-
franchising first men without property, then
African-Americans, then women; letting citizens
elect their own United States senators, and now
selecting candidates through direct primary elections rather than through political conventions. As
the unfamiliar became familiar, critics' fears were
forgotten and the republic endured.

In the conclusion of William Greider's recent
book, *Who Will Tell the People: The Betrayal of
American Democracy*, the author sounds an opti-
mistic note about the difficult evolution of American
democracy as he cites Vaclav Havel, the Czechoslo-
vakian playwright and former president who
describes genuine democracy as "a distant horizon
that no human society has yet reached or perhaps
ever will reach." Greider adds: "But that does not
end the story and, in some ways, the search in
America may be only just beginning."[26]

4

A Short History of Referendums

Referendums have their roots in early democratic practices of the ancient Greek city-states, as well as the Roman *plebiscita,* from which is derived the word "plebiscite," an alternate term for "referendum." Referendum, as defined earlier, is the practice of submitting a measure passed or proposed by a legislative body or citizens to a popular vote. At times a national referendum is advisory, a gauge of public opinion, but usually the result is binding on the government.

Reasons for Referendum

Governments can hold referendums for a variety of reasons. Generally, the public gets to decide public policy for one of three reasons—a constitutional necessity, a legitimizing function or a transfer of decision-making to the public.[1]

Constitutional Necessity. Many constitutions require referendums whenever a constitutional amendment is proposed. Australians, for example, cannot change their constitution without a referendum; consequently, 36 of their 39 national referendums have been on constitutional questions.[2]

Legitimizing Function. Referendums provide legitimacy on controversial decisions. Although representative governments have sufficient authority, certain decisions require a show of public support. Critics, who would have forever chastised the British Parliament for joining the European Economic Community (EEC), were largely silenced when more than two-thirds of British voters in a 1975 referendum supported continued participation in the EEC.[3] In 1992 some EEC member nations held referendums to confirm the Maastricht Treaty, which consolidates many functions of their separate national governments into a unified European whole. A mandate for such dramatic change is best secured by national referendum, not legislative decision.

Transfer of decision-making to the public. Often when politicians decide an issue has become too volatile, they pass it to the voters. Past examples include an Italian referendum on repealing divorce laws and military conscription referendums in Australia, Canada and New Zealand.[4]

Uses of Referendums

Despots sometimes use democratic mechanisms to create the illusion of public support and legitimacy for their governments. Napoleon Bonaparte and Napoleon III both justified their authority by frequently holding referendums. Adolf Hitler sought endorsement for his policies through plebiscites. Not satisfied with simple majorities, these authoritarian leaders claimed nearly unanimous approval by the voters.[5]

Referendums often prove to be a useful tool for peaceful territorial decisions. In 1905 Norwegians voted to separate from Sweden. After World War I eight League of Nations plebiscites provided national self-determination to various peoples. In 1967 Gibraltar voted to keep its ties with the United Kingdom.[6]

At times referendum voters make specific policy decisions. Citizens of Denmark, France and Ireland determined the legal voting age in their countries. In other countries voters have decided moral questions such as the role of the church or the legality of alcoholic beverages. Still other referendums have dealt with practical matters, such as pensions, rules of the road or land laws.[7]

With the exception of Switzerland, national referendums generally tend to be isolated events rather than part of a systematic effort to include voters in the legislative process.

Four Basic Types of Referendums

There are four basic types of referendums— government-controlled referendums, constitutionally required referendums, referendums by popular petitions and popular initiatives. Most nations allow for only the first, government-controlled referendums.[8]

Government-controlled referendums. Typically, a majority of the legislature decides to offer a specific question to voters and determines the wording, what percentage of affirmative votes are needed for approval and whether it will be advisory or binding on the government.

Constitutionally required referendums. When the legislature controls the content of amendments to the constitution and when they will be proposed, a referendum may be required by the constitution to guarantee voters the final say in whether the amendments are adopted. A constitution may also require referendums on non-constitutional measures, such as taxes.

Referendums by popular petitions. Some constitutions grant citizens the right to challenge a law already approved by the government. By obtaining a minimum number of signatures on a petition, the public can force the law to a popular vote. If the referendum voters do not approve the measure, it cannot become law.

Popular Initiatives. Some constitutions allow citizens to file a petition for a referendum on a resolution proposed by the citizens themselves. Where the government provides for indirect initiatives, the resolution first goes to the legislature. Where there are direct initiatives, citizens may enact or reject their own resolution by a popular vote, without the consent of the legislative or executive branches of government. Only the judicial branch may overrule the enacted law, strictly on constitutional grounds.

Referendums in Switzerland

Switzerland, which uses all four types of referendums, has held more nationwide referendums than any other country. From 1900 through September 1, 1978, there had been just over 500 nationwide referendums in the world, 297 in Switzerland.[9]

Switzerland has a history of allowing its citizenry to vote directly on important issues. As early as the Middle Ages, Bern and several other Swiss cantons used referendums for making decisions. When Switzerland became a federation in 1848 only constitutional amendments proposed by the government could be subjected to a referendum, but as of 1874 any federal statute could be referred to the people. The Swiss people themselves may initiate changes in their constitution and put them to a referendum vote.[10]

Under the current Swiss system all referendums are binding. A referendum must be held on a particular bill passed by the Federal Assembly if the populace can gather 50,000 signatures. It takes 100,000 signatures to propose an initiative. If a referendum issue fails to attain both a popular majority and a majority in more than half of the 22 cantons which comprise the Swiss nation, it cannot become law.[11]

Up to 1989 the Swiss had held over 300 referendums and proposed more than 135 initiatives on a wide range of issues:[12] weights and measures, religious liberty, copyrights, the death penalty, nationalization of a railway, federal income tax, gambling houses, protection of the family, federal finances, nuclear arms prohibition, milk and milk products, women's suffrage, air pollution from cars, education, pensions and health insurance. Resolutions on all these issues and many more have been put to the voters for their acceptance or rejection.[13]

Swiss legislators craft a law with public opinion in mind, hoping to avoid a citizen petition which could force a referendum on the law. The existence of the referendum process maintains a constant pressure on legislators to pass laws which please the people. When a law is challenged, an affirmative vote assures the legislature that people support what their lawmakers are doing. A negative vote, which happens fewer than once in three times,

forces the legislature to conform its efforts to public
opinion. Initiatives, which are normally promoted
by minority factions, have an extremely low rate of
approval. They do, however, foster greater public
awareness of unfamiliar matters.[14]

In recent years the Swiss have voted as many as
four times annually on various referendum questions, not including elections for public officials.
Voter participation has suffered somewhat during
the past 50 years, as it has in most modern industrial nations. Nonetheless, direct democracy has
enhanced Swiss political life without apparent negative consequences. Unlike any other place in the
world, citizen involvement in Switzerland is integral to the normal functioning of its representative
government.

*The Relationship between Switzerland and the
United States*

New England town meetings are similar to the
traditional Swiss *Landgemeinden*, annual open-air
meetings where all the men in a canton vote on local
government policies. Although appropriate for small
rural communities, town meetings in some parts of
New England, like most of the *Landgemeinden*,
disappeared with population growth, industrializa-
tion and urbanization. The spirit of town meetings
underlies the tradition of direct democracy in the
United States, as does the *Landgemeinde* in Switzerland.

In 1848 Switzerland became a federation modeled after the United States, with a bicameral Federal Assembly and a president. As in the American states, its 22 cantons are represented in the federal government.

After Switzerland began using initiative and referendum extensively to allow citizens to decide on laws, James W. Sullivan, a New York city labor theorist, went to study the Swiss system in 1888. His popular book, *Direct Legislation Through the Initiative and Referendum*, was one of the primary influences on the Progressive Era effort to adopt initiative and referendum in American state and local governments.[15]

Referendums in the United States

The United States has never held a nationwide referendum of any kind, not even an advisory referendum. Yet the United States has more experience with the various forms of referendum than any other nation, including Switzerland—on the state and local level.

The first constitutional referendums in history took place in some of the American colonies when they replaced their old colonial charters with new state charters. The Massachusetts legislature designed a constitution in 1778 which was overwhelmingly rejected in town meetings across the state. Not until 1780 did a two-thirds majority of Massachusetts citizens, again in town meetings, give approval to a new constitution drafted by a state constitutional convention. At about the same time New Hampshire's town assemblies also rejected a constitution, approving a redrafted constitution a few years later. Other states subsequently submitted their constitutions to referendums so that new states holding constitutional referendums became the accepted practice by the 1850s.[16]

Today 49 states require referendums on any amendments to their state constitutions. Only Delaware, which has never held any kind of binding referendum, lacks that requirement. In addition, 39 states permit some form of statutory referendum, 24 by petition of their citizens. ("Statutory" refers to ordinary laws, as opposed to constitutional issues.) And, 22 states provide for popular initiative by petition. Of those allowing popular initiative, 15 states provide for direct initiative, which puts the proposed measure directly onto the ballot for referendum. The other seven use the indirect initiative, whereby the measure goes to the legislature first. In most of the states using indirect initiative, if the legislature does not act within a certain period of time, the proposed measure then goes on the ballot for a referendum. In 39 states various kinds of referendums by local governments are permitted or required.[17]

Local governments in the United States hold 10,000-15,000 referendums annually. In recent years these referendums have most frequently involved public school tax and bond issues. Other local ballot issues, sometimes controversial, have ranged from fluoridation of municipal water to gay rights. Local referendums have been little examined by political scientists, although state initiatives and referendums have been the subject of a great deal of study.[18]

A compilation of state-level popular initiatives from 1898 to January 1, 1977, shows 539 referendums on constitutional amendments and 685 statutory referendums. During those eight decades, popular initiatives of both kinds have been most frequently employed by Oregon (207), California (159), North Dakota (137), Colorado (110) and Arizona (117).[19]

The greatest number of state initiatives (26 percent) were attempts to change government structures or political processes.[20] Many innovative state initiatives achieved reforms long before they became common practice or were adopted by the U.S. Constitution. Early state initiatives established nominations of candidates through primary elections, presidential primaries rather than state conventions, direct election of U.S. senators, recall of public officials, home rule for local governments and permanent voter registration. More than half a century before the U.S. Supreme Court required reapportionment of electoral districts based on population, a 1912 Arizona initiative mandated such reapportionment for the lower house of its state legislature. Initiatives in Arizona and Oregon achieved women's suffrage nine years before the

Nineteenth Amendment enfranchised all American women.[21]

The next most frequent use of state initiatives (21 percent) has involved revenue, taxation and bonds—measures to remove a state constitutional prohibition against a graduated income tax, for example, or a law to improve roads with gasoline tax revenues.[22]

The next two most common uses of state initiatives (both 14 percent) have been measures to regulate business and labor and proposals concerning public morality. Citizens have voted on changes in the regulation of electric utility charges or chiropractors, or changes in the state constitution to prohibit union membership as a precondition for employment (called "right to work" laws). They have decided whether alcoholic beverages may be sold and whether to establish a state lottery.[23]

The least common uses of initiatives, according to this compilation which ends in early 1977, have been in areas such as health, welfare and housing (9 percent), environmental protection and land use (7 percent), education (6 percent) and civil liberties and civil rights (3 percent).[24]

The use of popular initiatives in the states has ebbed and flowed. The newfound right to propose initiatives was frequently used during the Progressive Era. In 1914 an all-time high of 90 initiatives was proposed. Initiative use declined during both world wars but increased again after each conflict. In the postwar era of the '50s and '60s initiative use gradually dwindled to its all-time low of 10 in 1968. Between 1968 and 1982 popular initiatives increased by more than 600 percent in a resurgence that has continued to the present day.[25] State legislators also have placed many thousands of referendum issues on the ballot since the early 1900s. Of the constitutional changes proposed by legislators, 60.6 percent were approved by voters, compared with 34.5 percent for constitutional changes proposed by popular initiative. For statutory questions, the outcome was 60.1 percent and 38.1 percent.[26]

Whether popular initiatives favor liberal or conservative causes is an important question that is often raised. From 1945 to 1976, state initiatives that could clearly be identified as liberal or conservative, such as abortion on demand or the death penalty, were fairly evenly divided in results. Conservatives won 24 victories, liberals won 19.[27] A more recent assessment of state initiatives, from 1977 to 1988, produced similar results. Voters faced 96 ballot initiatives placed by liberal, environmentalist or left-leaning groups, approving 43 of them; they acted on 91 initiatives from conservative groups, approving 41 of them.[28]

Many issues cannot be readily identified in terms of traditional affiliations: Democrat or Republican, conservative or liberal. When faced with a specific question, particularly on a local level, ideological labels tend to blur. In a hotly contested referendum in 1983 in Bucks County, Pennsylvania, where I

live, voters challenged county commissioners on
their decision to build a pumping station to move
water from the Delaware River to a nuclear power
plant in another county. Many traditional conservatives found themselves on the same side of the
issue as long-haired, anti-nuclear protesters. The
referendum outcome, although only advisory, per-
suaded county commissioners to terminate
construction on the project.[29]

Electronic Democracy

No national, state or local government has ever
conducted a referendum using electronic technology, although there have been experiments in
"electronic town meetings" and "televoting."

A series of five electronic town meetings were
sponsored in 1976 by the New York Regional Plan
Association. There was wide media coverage with
18 television stations cooperating to broadcast the
meetings and 28 newspapers publishing mail-in
ballots. Only 120,000 people mailed in ballots out of
an estimated two million viewers.[30]

The "televote" system was demonstrated at the
University of Hawaii before delegates to that state's
constitutional convention in 1978. Through public
television, radio and newspapers, the demonstra-
tion project publicized certain issues under
discussion at the convention, providing the public
with detailed information on alternatives. The
project polled a random sample of citizens before

and after the media presentations, obtaining feedback and unofficial votes through telephone calls. Although proponents of the televote system aspire to a more integrated two-way technology combining presentation and polling, those who participated in the experiment favored the idea of televoting and liked being included.[31]

In the early 1980s Warner-Amex Cable Corporation's interactive television system, called "QUBE," was used for unofficial electronic referendums on municipal issues in several communities, including a suburb of Columbus, Ohio. When watching certain local government meetings broadcast on the cable network, citizens could push buttons on the console to indicate their opinions. Critics claim that the polled sample was not representative of the population, that there were no controls to keep children from voting and that the cost of subscribing imposed a sort of poll tax on citizens. The use of QUBE was discontinued in 1984.[32]

The city of Reading, Pennsylvania, in 1992 employed two-way television to allow conversation between city councilors in public meetings and citizens at home. People who cannot attend the meeting in person are still able to participate.[33]

Television networks, on occasion, have conducted informal telephone polls. ABC News encouraged viewers to call a 900-number to pick a winner after the first Carter-Reagan debate in 1980.[34] CBS conducted a viewer poll after President Bush's State of the Union address in January 1992. More than 20 million telephone calls were made in attempts to reach the national number CBS provided, but only 300,000 got through.[35] These informal polls are very crude measures of public opinion with the same limitations as the ill-fated QUBE system: the voting public is not accurately represented, there are no controls on who votes or how often and there is a cost associated with voting.

Conclusion

Two of the three reasons cited for holding referendums apply to the Electronic Congress. If heeded by congressmen, regularly held national referendums would legitimize legislative decisions and provide selective opportunities to transfer some decision-making directly to the public. Included in the legislative process, citizens would feel connected to their representatives.

Most of the issues on the Electronic Congress ballots would be government-controlled referendum questions. Congress would decide which binding and advisory questions could appear on the monthly or quarterly ballot. Only on an advisory basis would the Electronic Congress use popular initiative where citizens propose their questions for popular vote.

Switzerland, with fewer than seven million people, is only a tiny fraction of the size of the United States. Nonetheless, as a modern industrial society with a government modeled after that of the United

States, the Swiss use of referendums on a regular basis has implications for our own nation. The Swiss have demonstrated that a federal government can involve its citizens in the legislative process in a meaningful way. The Electronic Congress would be a modified version of the Swiss system, adapted to the unique needs of our own nation.

Referendums conducted throughout the United States illustrate our creativity as a free people. We and our elected representatives have developed an impressive variety of solutions to state and local problems. Our collective wisdom, including both liberal and conservative outlooks, could readily be applied to national affairs.

What sets the Electronic Congress concept apart from existing practices is the means by which the referendums would be conducted. Telephone voting would allow referendums to be held frequently and conveniently, once the system were in place. Telephone petitioning would also make it feasible for citizens to put their own ideas before the public and the legislature for consideration.

We can avoid the problems of early attempts at electronic democracy because we have the knowledge and technology to insure that all citizens have equal access to a secure voting system. We do not have to wait for two-way broadcasting or new electronic gadgets. As the precedent of the televote experiment in Hawaii suggests, the dissemination of useful and understandable information is more important than the sophistication of the voting technology. Informed and competent voters are the most critical element in an Electronic Congress.

5

Assessing Voter Competence

One of the concerns often expressed about the Electronic Congress is that voters are not competent to decide laws. Critics view the public as irrational, incapable of understanding complex issues, easily influenced by well-financed media campaigns and likely to trample on the rights of minorities. Their worst fear is that involving voters in the Congressional decision-making process would be disastrous for the nation. One critic wrote, "The fact remains that the body of voters is not at all equipped to understand even ordinary bills, and one of the chief failings of the referendum has been the inability of the voter to use it intelligently."[1]

Research and experience do not support this view. Betty H. Zisk, in a study of campaigns and

outcomes on major ballot questions in four states—
Massachusetts, Michigan, Oregon and California—from
1976 to 1982, reported that there was "very little
evidence for most of the common pessimistic lore about
voter confusion or negative voting."[2] A New York State
Senate committee in 1980 studied voter rationality in
ballot issue elections in many states. The majority
report of the committee concluded that voters were
surprisingly sophisticated in dealing with ballot questions, looking beyond their personal self-interest and
considering the overall well-being of their state and
society.[3]

California Proposition 13 and the Tax Revolt

If ever a referendum issue raised concerns about
voter rationality, it was California's "Proposition
13." On June 6, 1978, a majority of California's
voters (64.8 percent) approved a tax cut initiative
which amended the state constitution. The amendment limited property taxes to one percent of assessed
value and allowed tax bills to increase by only two
percent annually. Much to the dismay of California
government officials and legislators, property taxes
were reduced by an average of 57 percent, an overall
tax cut of $6 billion, about one-sixth of California
state and local government revenues.[4]

But the reasons for initiating Proposition 13
were not irrational. California residential property
values had experienced dramatic inflation during
the '60s and '70s and so had property taxes. Until

Proposition 13, properties were subject to reassessment whenever a neighboring house was sold for a higher value. Elderly homeowners on fixed incomes were often driven from their homes by taxes which doubled and sometimes tripled in less than five years. Howard Jarvis, a retired businessman, began his efforts to curb the dramatic increase in property taxes in 1968. Despite several failed petition drives, he and his allies, with the support of thousands of volunteers, finally gathered 1.2 million signatures and put the tax-cut initiative on the ballot for the primary election in the late spring of 1978.

Proposition 13 was opposed by public employee unions and state and local officials. The "No on 13" campaign raised more than $2 million. The legislature, hoping to persuade voters to accept a milder measure than Proposition 13, added Proposition 8 to the ballot which cut real estate taxes to a lesser extent and raised property taxes on business to make up for some of the cuts. Proposition 8 was not approved by the voters.

The "No on 13" campaign claimed that the proposed tax cuts would cost a half million jobs and gut local government services. Jarvis said that there was a $6 billion-$7 billion state surplus which could be contributed to help local governments absorb the cut in property taxes. Most state officials said there was only $1 billion-$2 billion. The surplus later turned out to be $7.3 billion.

The victory was achieved with majorities in both

political parties, every income and education group, and 55 of California's 58 counties. So strong was the anti-tax message delivered by the voters that the legislature subsequently cut state income taxes by $1 billion.

Across the nation, legislators and government officials feared that the widely publicized California tax revolt would create a voter stampede. They envisioned out-of-control citizens cutting government services and taxes, particularly in those states where popular initiatives gave the public direct access to decision-making.

When the so-called "tax revolt" reached South Dakota in 1980, James A. Meader, a political scientist studying voter behavior in that election, concluded: ". . . the voters are capable of taking a long-range view when they consider initiatives on the ballot . . . The voters evidenced a fairly high degree of sophistication and an ability to differentiate the issue on the ballot. South Dakotans voted down a tax cut . . . ."[5]

The tax revolt itself, often cited as an argument against citizen referendums, has been wildly exaggerated. Although a substantial number of major tax-cut initiatives were proposed in states from 1978 to 1984, voters were very selective. Out of the 19 proposals for tax cuts in 10 states, only three passed.[6] Even in California, of five major tax-cut initiatives on the ballot between 1968 and 1984, the voters approved only one. Yet the voters' support of Proposition 13 effectively warned California legisla-

tors and other lawmakers around the nation that
the voting public would not tolerate unlimited tax
increases.

Voter Weaknesses in Referendums

The initiative and referendum have not dra-
matically increased interest in public affairs, as the
Progressives predicted. James W. Sullivan, in his
1893 book, *Direct Legislation Through the Initiative
and Referendum*, said that "the sphere of every
citizen would be enlarged; each would consequently
acquire education in his role, and develop a lively
interest in the public affairs . . . ."[7]

Instead, better educated and more affluent voters are the citizens most likely to vote in elections,
both for candidates and for referendum issues. Those
with the greatest interest in the political system see
themselves as its beneficiaries. Less educated voters, members of lower socio-economic groups, and
minorities are the least likely to vote in elections.[8]

Less educated and poorer voters have particular
difficulty with complex and lengthy ballot issues.
They are often intimidated and fail to vote, even for
measures such as the 1976 Massachusetts graduated income tax, which would have benefited them
directly.[9]

Referendum questions sometimes confuse voters. Of the voters interviewed about a 1976 ballot
question on nuclear power plants, 14 percent had
inadvertently voted contrary to their stated inten-

tions. The greatest confusion is caused by questions
which are worded awkwardly, so that voters must
vote "yes" for what they oppose and vote "no" for
what they support. Such a question in California in
1980 caused a majority of those who wanted to
abolish rent control to vote against their preference.[10]

An important aid to addressing these voter weaknesses in an Electronic Congress would be
informative voting guides. Citizens now often rely
on pamphlets provided by the League of Women
Voters or by the states themselves.[11] One problem
is that states either do not provide guides or they are
written in impenetrable prose. An assessment of
readability levels of voting guides from various
states revealed that they are often written at the
reading level of a third-year college student. By
comparison, the study showed that *Time, Newsweek,
People* and *Reader's Digest* are written at reading
levels between ninth and twelfth grades.[12] Newspapers and magazines could probably do a better job of
developing voting guides than governments and
might include them as inserts in their regular publications. Well-written voting guides, with the
readability of popular literature, would improve
voter understanding of ballot questions.

The Electronic Congress would be less complicated for voters than general elections because
referendum questions would not be on the same
ballot as candidates running for office. In general
elections, ballot questions rarely get as much atten-

tion as the candidates. Voters usually focus first on which candidates they will vote for, then decide the ballot questions on the eve of the election.[13] Participants in the Electronic Congress would deal only with ballot questions.

Referendum Voters and Campaign Spending

One of the greatest fears of political scientists concerning ballot-question campaigns is that one-sided spending will unduly influence voters. In Betty H. Zisk's four-state study, money seemed to be a significant factor. In 56 of 72 ballot-question campaigns from 1976 to 1982, the bigger spending side won 78 percent of the time.[14]

Other assessments suggest that big money has only about a 25 percent success rate in promoting ballot issues which serve business or corporate interests. When it comes to blocking ballot issues, however, big money has a 75 percent chance of success, especially when opponents have a lot more money than proponents.[15] It is easier to raise doubts about a proposal than to sell one. A massive negative advertising campaign, particularly in the last days of the campaign, can exploit the natural tendency of voters to vote "no" when they are unsure. Voter confusion may kill the proposal unless backers have the money to respond quickly and effectively.

A factor which would help offset some of the effects of negative advertising in national referendums is that both the voting public and the news media pay more attention to national issues than to state and local issues. The information available to participants in the Electronic Congress would probably be greater than for most state ballot questions. Creative feature programs and articles in the broadcast and print media could help educate the voting public, reducing the influence of misinformation and exaggeration which characterize paid political advertising in election campaigns.

David D. Schmidt, an advocate of direct democracy, says that the impact of one-sided campaign funding is not significant. "Of the 189 state-level Initiative campaigns during the years 1976-1984 for which spending data is available, (about three-quarters of all campaigns during this period) campaign spending can be judged the decisive factor in only about 23—one-eighth of the total."[16]

Political scientists disagree with each other on this issue because identifying the primary factor in a ballot-question campaign is not easy. Many variables can influence the outcome: the voting public's inherent beliefs or prejudices, endorsements by individuals, organizations and political parties, effectiveness of print and broadcast advertising, perceived integrity of proponents and opponents, campaign organization, availability of volunteers. Money is only one of the variables, although unquestionably an important one.

Apparently the role of money is not important enough for the U.S. Supreme Court to allow states to prohibit or limit corporate contributions or spending in initiative campaigns. Controversial Supreme Court decisions overruled most of the laws limiting corporate spending which had been in effect in 18 states.

The most significant decision was the *Belloti* case in 1978 which challenged a Massachusetts law prohibiting corporations from financially supporting ballot-question campaigns not materially affecting their businesses. In ruling against that law, the U.S. Supreme Court, by a vote of only five to four, maintained that corporations also have First Amendment rights to freedom of speech and may fund campaigns for or against ballot issues.

Attorneys representing Francis Belloti, attorney general for the Commonwealth of Massachusetts, argued that financial domination of ballot-question campaigns by corporate money might undermine the voters' faith in the democratic process. The Supreme Court majority ruled that "there has been no showing that the relative voice of corporations has been overwhelming or even significant in influencing referenda in Massachusetts, or that there has been any threat to the confidence of the citizenry in government." [17]

Since the *Belloti* decision in 1978, most research suggests that voters might be unduly influenced by one-sided spending.[18] But until that research conclusively influences a future Supreme Court decision, states must refrain from placing restrictions on corporate funding in ballot issues. Despite that handicap, Schmidt contends that the merits of ref-

erendums outweigh the detriment of big money
influence on voters. "Even assuming that money
had a decisive effect on defeated initiatives where
there was one-sided opposition spending . . . Are
voters to be prevented from voting on *all* initiatives
just because they exhibit massive opposition to *some*
initiatives? To do so would be analogous to abolish-
ing candidate races because third-party candidates
so rarely get elected." [19]

Comparing Voters with Legislators

In evaluating voter competence to decide ballot
questions, there are surely weaknesses to be found.
The underlying question is whether voters are any
less capable of deciding laws than legislators. Too
often opponents of the referendum process demean
the voter while they hold the legislator on a pedes-
tal.

Critics, for example, express concern that voter
participation in direct democracy will tyrannize
minorities. It is true that voters have occasionally
violated minority rights. In 1920 Californians approved a discriminatory initiative which limited the
right of Japanese people to own land. But more
often they have defeated such ballot measures as,
for example, the 1978 California initiative restricting gay rights. Legislatures also have discriminated
against minorities, restricting their voting rights,
imposing censorship or loyalty oaths and forbidding
the teaching of certain subjects. Citizens voting on

ballot questions are no more prone to abridge freedoms or limit the rights of minorities than legislatures.[20]

Although voters are accused of being too easily influenced by campaign spending, big money has clearly influenced legislators in Congress and state legislatures. Political action committees contribute vast sums to candidate campaigns, so much so that corruption in the legislative process has become a national crisis. Ken Thompson, director of Citizens for Participation in Political Action, in testifying before a U.S. Senate committee, said that "the corrupting effect of money on ballot questions is the lesser of evils compared to its effect on candidate campaigns."[21] At least the money in ballot-question campaigns is spent on persuading voters, not on buying special favors.

Other opponents of referendums claim that society has become too complicated for amateur lawmakers. Supposedly being full-time professionals gives legislators a tremendous advantage over citizens in studying the bills which come before them. But Senator Kent Conrad's (D-South Dakota) perception of daily life in Congress does not support that:

"As far as I'm concerned, the real problem here is time or the lack of it. As I left for home the other evening at 7 o'clock, which is usually the case, I looked back on the day and decided it was typical: meetings with constituents from home, fund raising, committee meetings. I came to Washington because

I was deeply concerned about the deficit.... I'm also very concerned about education and health care ... But none of those things got a moment of thought or attention that day." [22]

Legislators specialize in their areas of interest, relying on colleagues and staff to help them make decisions in other areas. Similarly, voters rely on friends and the media to help them make decisions about ballot questions. In reality, most issues are decided by choosing among competing values and interests. Even those who are not engaged in lawmaking on a full-time basis can make those kinds of discriminations.

Furthermore, legislators do not necessarily represent the best interests of their state or nation. Unsavory legislative practices are so commonplace that they have acquired colorful names. Legislators "gerrymander" voting districts, manipulating boundaries to protect their own political party's candidates for re-election. They "logroll" votes, exchanging support for each other's bills without consideration of their merits. Such bills often consist of funding for unnecessary projects in the legislator's home district, called "pork barrel" legislation, which favors particular groups of constituents at the expense of the general taxpayer. Legislators often sneak through their pet proposals, known as "cats and dogs," at times when legislative activity is frantic and confused. [23]

One such frantic and confused time was described by an eyewitness in the Virginia legislature in 1984, only in this case legislators were killing bills without considering their merits: "It was the night of the long knives. Good bills, bad bills, almost 200 of them rolled through the Virginia General Assembly's House Courts of Justice Committee .... With cries of 'PBI' (pass by indefinitely) ringing through the air—a euphemism for kill the bill—the 20-member executive committee performed its tasks with great relish. And, as the night progressed and patience wore thin, the panel's thirst for sending legislation to the graveyard increased .... 'I've been down here 17 years and I'm still baffled by what they do,' said Fairfax Republican Delegate Vincent F. Callahan, Jr .... 'Nobody else understands the bills. Even the lawyers don't understand them.' "[24]

William Greider, in *Who Will Tell the People*, relates an experience he had as a young reporter covering the Kentucky state legislature: "In the midst of debate, the legislators erupted in noisy chaos—shouting wildly at one another and throwing papers in the air, charging randomly around the House chamber like angry children in a group tantrum."[25]

I do not mean to discredit representative democracy by citing these practices and examples. My purpose in proposing the Electronic Congress is to strengthen representative democracy. Those critics who dismiss voters as incapable of deciding on laws need to set aside their illusions and remember that both legislators and their constituents sometimes make mistakes, get confused, act out of emotion,

violate minority rights, lack time for careful delib-
eration and are influenced by money. Legislators
are only people with flaws just like the "folks back
home" who elect them.

Conclusion

Voters have demonstrated competence and sometimes sophistication in referendums. By comparison
with legislators, they are no more likely to limit
minority rights or respond to the influence of money.
While some legitimate concerns may be raised about
the power of big money in ballot-question campaigns, voters tend to err on the side of caution.
They are more easily influenced to vote "no" than to
approve a change in the law. Even the fear of tax
revolts has proved unfounded.   In the case of
California's famous Proposition 13, there was a
legitimate need for tax relief. But the overall record
of direct democracy in the American states shows
that voters have been responsible and prudent in
their decisions.
The fact that ballot-question voters tend to be
more educated and more affluent than the average
citizen is not a problem. They are far more representative of the public than the average legislator—a
white, middle-aged, male lawyer.[26] Besides, voters
who do not participate in referendums, particularly
on complex ballot questions, are *choosing* not to
vote. Presumably they abstain because they are
unsure or uninterested. This does not mean that

they will not vote later when they acquire knowledge or opinions about the ballot questions. Their choice to abstain is not irrational because they are choosing to delegate the decision to their fellow citizens.

Voters have been entrusted with the task of selecting legislators. That the republic has endured more than 200 years is adequate testament to their competence. If voters are competent to choose their representatives, then they are competent to help choose their laws.

6

Telephone-Voting
Technology

The Electronic Congress would not rely on the existing system established by the states for voting in elections because that would limit citizen participation to one referendum each spring and fall. National referendums would be held more often, perhaps monthly or quarterly, and to do this, the federal government would establish an independent telephone voting system.

The idea of telephone voting, to supplement or replace voting machines in regular elections, is not new.

"The idea turns up with a regularity that is truly astonishing," said Bill Kimberling, deputy director of the Federal Election Commission's National Clearinghouse on Election Administration. "I think these people have been watching Star Trek a little too much." Kimberling's remarks appeared in a 1991 newspaper article about the Voting by Phone Foundation, which was trying to legalize phone voting in regular elections in Boulder, Colorado, by 1994.

He said, "We looked into it and concluded that, even if it were technologically feasible, the cost of the technology would far exceed whatever benefit might accrue." And, Kimberling argued, telephone voting would not be more convenient: "I'm not sure that spending thirty minutes listening to directions and punching buttons on the phone is making voting easier."

Kimberling expressed other concerns, stating that telephone voting risked voter fraud, lacked privacy and would be subject to sabotage by computer hackers. "How would you be sure someone wasn't standing next to the caller telling him how to vote? " he asked. "There are just too many flaws." [1]

Kimberling's statements revealed a lack of thoughtful consideration. The telephone has been around for 100 years and the computer for 40. He spoke as if proponents of telephone voting were advocating a futuristic concept, like "beaming up" to spaceships, but telephone voting is based on established technology.

"There's no doubt in my mind that a cost-effective, user-friendly system could be designed," said Joseph Pelton, director of the University of Colorado's graduate telecommunications program and technical adviser to the Voting by Phone Foundation.

"Remember that, twenty years ago, people thought it would be crazy to trust your money to a bank machine; now everybody uses them."[2]

"Technical people are confident it will work and that the bugs can be worked out," said Evan Ravitz, founder and director of the Voting by Phone Foundation. "It's the non-technical people who are afraid of it."[3]

Voting by telephone in the Electronic Congress would be similar to many business applications already in use on a daily basis throughout the United States. Important transactions are commonly carried out by the interaction of computers and private telephones. College students register for courses and pay their tuition with credit cards. Bank customers access their accounts and pay bills. They do so by entering Touch-Tone signals in response to digitized computer voices without any college or bank personnel participating in the process. This technology can easily be adapted to telephone voting.

Perhaps unaware that voting by telephone could be streamlined through the use of coordinated print materials, Kimberling overstated the time involved in telephone voting. With guides that prepare voters before they call, the voting-system computer voice would not have to explain directions or list all the choices for ballot questions. Directions and choices would be provided in writing, along with appropriate Touch-Tone number for each choice on each ballot question. When voters phoned, the computerized voice would simply name each ballot question and await the Touch-Tone response. Voting by telephone would take a couple of minutes.

Kimberling failed to consider the hassle of going to the polls. He forgot the time voters spend traveling to and from, standing in line, waiting to enter the voting booth. He forgot the speculation before each Election Day about how the weather might affect turnout. Placing a telephone call is more convenient, especially for older voters and those who work.

As Americans consider a new voting technology, they should acknowledge fears about voter fraud, sabotage and other potential problems, but before dismissing the proposal, as Kimberling was quick to do, they should compare it to the existing system, which often is accepted without question.

Voter registration now usually operates on an honor system. New registrants state their names and addresses without showing identification. Many people register by mail. They are usually asked to swear in writing that the information they provide is true. On Election Day, voters reconfirm their names and addresses at the polls, often without showing their registration cards. When voters move to a new home, they must re-register. Sometimes voting officials at the new location will notify the voting officials at the old location about the change, but not always. Presumably each voter votes only once at only one location, although many elections have been won with the votes of people long deceased.

Voter registration for the Electronic Congress would be simpler. Each voter would be assigned a 13-digit voter identification number once in a lifetime. Voters would not re-register when they move; instead, they would request their identification number be assigned to the new district. The identification number could be assigned to only one location at a time.

Registrants could use their Social Security numbers plus a four-digit code to create a unique 13-digit voter identification number. Most people have already memorized their Social Security numbers. Four-digit codes are commonplace for bank cards so registrants could adopt one that they already use. The combination would be easy to remember.

With respect to the security of the 13-digit number, it is one of 10 trillion possibilities. Even if a person learned someone else's Social Security number, that person would have only a one in 10,000 chance of guessing the four-digit code and voting in place of the other individual.

Voter privacy was another issue raised by Kimberling, although the nature of his concern was not made clear in the article. Perhaps his concern was that the computer would in some way violate voter privacy, but the computer would only function like a voting machine at the polls. It would not record the votes of individual voters, only totals of votes. For voter registration purposes and recounts, as is the current practice, there would also be a paper record maintained of which registered voters participated in each election and the votes cast on each ballot issue.

If Kimberling's concern was that someone might stand next to telephone voters while they vote, why was he not concerned about absentee ballots which entail the same risk? Although our current voting system has potential for fraud, everyone now assumes that abuse occurs very rarely. With phone voting, as with the existing system, it would be difficult to engage in an extensive vote-buying scheme without attracting attention and risking the penalties provided by laws against bribing and coercing voters.

Any large-scale, systematic invasion of voter privacy would require widespread use of wiretaps, but the growing utilization of fiber optic cable for telephone communication will soon make wiretapping impossible. Even the F.B.I. lacks the capability to tap fiber optic phone lines.[4] Furthermore, why would anyone want to go to all that trouble to find out how others voted? Pollsters may be interested in how people vote, but who else would be in a position to benefit from such information?

Kimberling displayed his lack of technical knowledge when he cited the danger of sabotage from computer hackers. The voting-system computer would allow people to communicate only in Touch-Tone numbers. Unless the voting computer has a provision for authorized programmers to access the system by telephone, it is impossible for unauthorized programmers to access the system by telephone to sabotage computer software.

Anyone worried about whether all voters have telephones, particularly Touch-Tone telephones, can be assured that 93 percent of American households have telephones. People who do not should be able to use someone else's for a few minutes. The voting-system computer might be made to accommodate dial or pulse telephones, but that probably is not necessary. Most new dial phones include an optional capability to generate Touch-Tones. Using conventional pulse dialing, voters without Touch-Tone service can reach the voting system, then switch to Touch-Tone to indicate their choices to the computer. There are also devices which can be held to the mouthpiece of a telephone to produce Touch-Tones.

Kimberling was correct in warning that telephone lines would be overwhelmed by too many calls made at one time. In 1991, when Pepsi Cola planned a million-dollar giveaway on nationwide television at half-time during the Super Bowl, the Federal Communications Commission, at the urging of AT&T, warned Pepsi's management that a massive response would shut down the nation's phone system. Pepsi canceled its plans.[5]

The Electronic Congress could avoid such problems by spreading referendum voting over a longer time period, perhaps a couple of days, and by dispersing calls to computer-voting centers in different parts of the country.

Another concern expressed by Kimberling was the cost of telephone voting. An electronic voting system is affordable, even for local government. A small two-line system, which could handle close to 60 two-minute voting calls an hour, would cost about $5,000 to establish. A larger 24-line system, which could handle more than 700 two-minute calls an hour, would cost about $20,000.[6] By extrapolation, a national system to accommodate 100 million voters would cost $50 million-$100 million.

A municipality might opt to contract for telephone voting services. For an initial programming fee of about $500, a telephone service bureau could provide local government with electronic voting capabilities. The cost for each referendum would be a few hundred dollars and about 10 cents per call.[7] On a national basis, the federal government would have to provide 800-line service so that voters would avoid long-distance telephone call charges.

The cost of the Electronic Congress voting system compares favorably with present voting technology. Purchasing, storing, insuring, maintaining and transporting voting machines is expensive. So is the cost of establishing polling places, staffing them with officials and updating voter-registration records for two elections each year.

The first use of voting machines for an election in the United States occurred in 1892 in Lockport, New York. Although each voting machine was expensive compared to paper ballots, it eventually

paid for itself by requiring fewer election officials
and less printing for each election. Despite the
economy and increased privacy afforded by voting
machines, the public was slow to accept them. Politicians and government officials fought against their
use and expressed fears and doubts, not unlike
those expressed by Bill Kimberling of the Federal
Election Commission about telephone voting.

Voting machines can continue to be used for
general elections even if the Electronic Congress is
implemented for national referendums. When voting by phone becomes commonplace, fears and doubts
will subside. In June 1992 in Nova Scotia, Canada,
the Liberal Party held a province-wide telephone
vote to select its new leader, a step which observers
say compels the other political parties to do the
same thing. In late July the U.S. House Subcommittee on Elections heard testimony on allowing phone
or fax voting for overseas civilians and military
personnel. During the Gulf War soldiers in the
Mideast were allowed to vote by fax.[8] Sooner or later
we will find ourselves phoning in our votes for
candidate elections as well, with telephone voting
accepted as a normal part of the political process.

7

Imagining the Process

The Electronic Congress, by involving the public in important decisions, would change the dynamics of national government. To gain an understanding of those changes, I found myself trying to imagine how legislators might behave in an Electronic Congress:

"Excuse me, Luke. I think you'll want to take this phone call. It's Charlie Williams. Can you talk now?"

Representative Henry Lucas looked up from his reading with a frown. A 14-year veteran of the House, "Luke," as his friends called him, would be facing a strong election challenge in November. More than ever, he was trying to keep everyone happy.

Charlie Williams was the chief lobbyist for the Committee for American Defense, one of the most influential political action committees (PACs) in Washington.

"I assume he's calling me about 122."

"Yep. I think all the media coverage has him worried that 122 is finally going to get out of committee."

"Which line is he on?"

"Line three."

"Hello, Charlie. How are you, fella?"

"Fine, Luke, real fine. How about yourself?"

"Good. I haven't seen you since the Spragues' party. Must be two weeks. Where have you been keeping yourself?"

"Been real busy. House Resolution 122's been getting a lot of press and air time lately, so I've been working real hard."

"I can imagine. You know how I feel about keeping those bases open. But I'm getting a lot of mail from my constituents in favor of closing them."

"I realize that. The bill's backers are trying to create the impression that there's a lot of public support, but our research shows otherwise. And 122 will eliminate over fifty thousand jobs, a thousand in your own district when Fort Warner closes."

"Charlie, you know I've always been for a strong military. I've voted to keep this issue in committee for the last six years . But there's starting to be a lot of talk about putting this one on the Electronic Congress ballot. PBS featured an hour documentary last month on whether there are too many military bases *and* Time *did a two-page article a couple of weeks ago."*

"I hope you'll hang tough with us. I still think we can stop the bill from getting out of committee. If it goes to a referendum vote, supporters will spread a lot of lies and try to confuse the public in hopes of getting it passed."

"I hear you, and I'll support you as long as I can. I certainly wouldn't vote for the bill on its merits, but if it keeps getting media exposure, it will probably go to a referendum vote."

"We'd like to avoid that."

"I'll certainly do my part as committee chairman."

"That's all I can ask, Luke. I appreciate your support."

"Keep me posted."

"I'll do that, Luke. Thanks again."

Charlie Williams hung up the telephone.

"He's still with us, Ed. At least for now. He'll try to hold the line on 122 in his committee. But if he's outvoted in committee, he'll probably go along with the vote for a referendum. I think he's under a lot of pressure from other PACs."

"And if 122 is referred out of committee, what do we do?"

"Well, if it gets to the floor we're going to try to keep it from being watered down with amendments to close fewer bases."

"What? I don't understand."

"Our polls tell us that a weaker version, closing

*fewer bases, is more likely to pass a referendum vote.
We don't want to see any amendments or changes if
the House brings it up for the Electronic Congress. A
strong version, closing all 31 of the targeted bases,
will turn off a lot of undecided voters."*

*"That's a big gamble, isn't it?   Kind of all or
nothing?"*

"I think it's our best shot if it goes on the ballot."

"I sure hope you know what you're doing."

*"I hope so, too, Ed.   At any rate, I think we can
count on Luke's support in committee.   And he'll help
us fend off amendments."*

"Did he say he'd do that?"

*"No, but he will. He doesn't like the idea of closing
bases and he'll support our strategy."*

*Luke finished his drink and put the glass down
with a sigh.*

*"I got a call from Charlie Williams today, Dick.
He's heading up the effort against House Resolution
122 and is really concerned that it will come out of
committee and go public."*

*"How come you feel so strongly about the bases?"
asked Luke's long-time friend, Representative Richard Prizinski. "Ever since we won the cold war a lot
of military analysts have questioned having so many
bases at home."*

*"I just don't buy that, Dick.   There are still
countries out there that would like to see the American military shrink.   If we let our guard down, who
knows what will happen?"*

"But you told me that even with Fort Warner in your own district, there's support for closing the base there. I think the public has a right to a referendum."

"Maybe you're right. If it gets out of committee, I'll probably support a referendum when it gets to the floor. I'm just nervous about going up against Charlie Williams. He's the last of the die-hards. He'll still be fighting 122 while the President is signing it into law. Aren't you concerned about Williams?"

"Not really. Williams is the kind of guy you can never satisfy. Even when you support him, a couple of weeks later he wants to know, 'What have you done for me lately?' "

"Don't I know it?" Luke sighed again.

I envisioned legislators using the advisory referendum votes to assess support for proposed bills on less controversial issues:

"We're not ready to push for a vote to get the issue out of committee yet. We don't have any idea how the public feels about tax credits for urban enterprise zones or which version of the bill has a chance of passing, either in the Senate or by referendum."

Senator Alice Lupo and her two staff members nodded their heads in acknowledgement.

"Tom, I agree with you completely," said Lupo to her colleague Senator Thomas Quinn. "Right now there are three versions in committee and I think we should send up a trial balloon by putting the options

into some advisory questions. I think we'll get some strong public support for enterprise zones but I'm not sure for which version."

"That's exactly my feeling, Alice. But I think some of our colleagues are pushing too fast. We need to assess the situation first."

Roger Goldberg, one of Quinn's staff, interrupted.

"Some senators want this bill passed in time for their primary elections back home. They want to show city voters what they're doing for them. I agree with having an advisory question vote before the bill comes out of committee, but it will be to our advantage if we can do it quickly."

"How quickly can we do it, Roger? Can we have advisory questions ready this week?"

"I'm sure we can. Susan already has a rough draft that we like and we can review them right now."

"Good, then let's prepare a resolution. We'll put them on the March referendum so we'll have a better idea where we stand for our next move."

I imagined voter participation in the Electronic Congress, assuming that some citizens would be excited by the opportunity and others would not:

Several days later the television set above the bar in a neighborhood tavern announced the news: "Today House Resolution 122, which mandates the closing of 31 military bases in the United States, was approved for referendum by a wide margin in the House. The next Electronic Congress referendum

*will be Friday, March 10, and Saturday, March 11.
Public opinion polls show a close vote on 122. Some
supporters say that the bill would have a better
chance of approval if it did not shut down so many
bases at one time. Opponents are expected to wage a
strong campaign against the bill. Six Senate advisory questions will also be on the referendum ballot."*

"Who gives a damn?"

A young man turned away from the television set,
complaining to the older man sitting next to him at
the bar.

"Do you ever vote on any of these things, Willy?"

"As a matter of fact I do."

"Do you? Well, I never have. I don't trust
politicians and I think this Electronic Congress
thing is just crap."

"Why's that?"

"I just don't trust politicians."

"I don't trust them either. That's why I vote in the
Electronic Congress. It gives me a say I never had
before. I voted for years in elections and never
thought it did any good, but I've voted in these
referendums and almost all the things I've voted for
have won. I think it's great."

"Well, I still think it's crap."

Elsewhere, three women were listening to radio
news at lunchtime.

"How are you voting on 122?" one woman asked
her colleagues.

"I'm not. You two are into it, but I don't have time

*for all that political stuff with two small kids to take
care of."*

*"Oh, Ellen, I know exactly how you feel. I remem-
ber when my kids were small. I never voted. But I
love the Electronic Congress. It's so easy to vote by
phone. Every month I read up on the issues, watch
a lot of interviews and special reports, and then I fill
out my voting guide. I feel like I'm really helping to
run the country. I love it."*

*"Did you see Congressman Harlan the other night
on Larry King's show?"*

"Oh, isn't he cute?"

*"Yeah, but he ticks me off. I don't agree with him
at all."*

*"What about Alice Lupo, the senator from New
Jersey? Did you see her going up against that
columnist?"*

*"I like her. I think she has her act together. She
rattles off facts without any notes and she always
keeps her sense of humor. I hope she runs for
President."*

*"My husband hates her. He thinks she's always
for big business and against the little guy."*

*"No way. I think she's a great senator. What did
you think of what she said about those enterprise
zones? I think it's a good idea for helping the cities."*

*"Well, I agree, but don't tell my husband how you
feel. You won't be able to shut him up."*

"Hey, did you sign the child-support initiative?"

"What's that?"

"It's only been listed on the Electronic Congress

*for a week or so. It asks if people want a federal law
to collect child support from men who've skipped the
state where their kids live?"*

"How did you find out about it?"

"I got something in the mail."

*"Bring it in for me to read. Maybe I'll call in and
get my husband to call in, too."*

*"Don't let him see the mailer 'cause Senator
Lupo's quoted in support of the petition."*

*"Hey, I'm sick of all this political talk. Don't you
two ever see any good movies?"*

Information on the issues could come from paid
commercials on both sides:

*The black screen slowly brightened into a sunrise
accompanied by a crescendo of dramatic orchestral
music with a deep-voiced narrator speaking.*

*"They claim it will be the dawning of a bright new
day..."*

*The picture cut to a large military base under a
gray sky. The image slowly widened its view to
include the front gate and then moved to a close-up
showing a sign on the gate which read "Closed" as the
music suddenly dragged to a halt.*

*"...but for the workers who lost their jobs here, it
is a dark day."*

*The image shifted to the interior of an unemploy-
ment office with long lines of jobless workers. Words
appeared on the screen which matched the narra-
tion.*

"House Resolution 122 will cost 50,000 Americans their jobs."

"VOTE NO on House Resolution 122."

Charlie Williams aimed the remote control and pressed the button to stop the videotape recorder.

"What do you think, Ed?"

"I think nobody's going to accuse us of being too subtle."

They both laughed.

"The other commercial hits the dangers of weakening our military strength."

"What's the broadcast schedule?"

"We're not putting anything on the air until the last week before the referendum. On March 6 this and our other ad will appear every half hour on prime time and almost every hour during the day on all the major networks and cable channels."

"Why wait until the last week?"

"We'd like to concentrate our commercials in the last week to get the most impact."

"Do you think 122 supporters will do the same?"

"No, they've already started some spots."

"Oh, I haven't seen them."

"That's exactly the point, Ed. Unless commercials are concentrated you can miss some viewers. And, the pro-122 commercials can't respond to our commercials if they don't appear until the last few days. Most voters make up their minds in the last few days anyway."

"Sounds good, Charlie."

Besides commercials sponsored by special interest groups trying to influence public opinion, people would get their information through television, newspapers, magazines and voting guides:

"We are pleased to have with us two highly respected national legislators, Congressman Richard Prizinski and Congressman Henry Lucas, both from California. Tonight they will be representing opposing views on House Resolution 122, a bill which proposes closing 31 domestic military bases. The issue will be decided in next week's Electronic Congress. I am Louis Perez, and welcome to 'Face to Face.'"

The two legislators, on either side of the moderator, smiled and nodded in response.

"I understand that the two of you are old friends."

"That's right, Lou," Dick Prizinski began. "We grew up in neighboring communities near San Francisco."

"And, we're used to being opponents," interjected Luke. "Our high schools played football against each other."

"You do go back a long way. We hope you'll feel that competitive spirit tonight and make vigorous arguments on this legislation. First, we have a videotaped introduction to help define the purpose of the proposed bill, House Resolution 122."

The video presentation gave background on the arguments for and against closing domestic military bases. Dick spoke up immediately.

"Lou, I have to take issue with your introductory video presentation. It implies that the supporters of this bill do not favor a strong military. Those of us who support House Resolution 122 recognize the need for a strong defense, but we believe that these bases are obsolete and serve no valid military purpose."

"Congressman, what do you say to that?"

"I disagree. These bases are the backbone of our reserve defenses. I don't want to see us face a crisis without the ability to mobilize quickly. Keeping these bases open is simply one of the costs of military preparedness, even if they don't seem necessary at the moment."

Bill watched "Face to Face," while his wife Jane read her voting guide.

"Bill, have you read this yet?"

"Shh, honey, I'm trying to hear this. It's almost over."

"O. K. Sorry."

Bill watched intently as the two legislators made their closing remarks and Louis Perez bid his viewers, "Good evening."

"Great show, Jane. Those two guys really got into it. I'm a little overwhelmed. They both were so passionate."

"That's why I like the voting guide. A lot less passionate but a lot more information."

"Have you decided how you're voting yet?"

"Well, I know I'm voting for House Resolution

122. I can't see saving jobs as a justification for wasting money on obsolete bases. I'm not sure on the advisory questions yet. I want to read some more articles. How about you?"

"I think I'm skipping the advisory questions. I don't really care about them."

"How about 122?"

"I'm with you, Jane. I hate their TV ads showing the closed base. I feel like they're using scare tactics."

"Want to look at the voting guide?"

"Nah, it's boring."

"Well, you might prefer the voting guide in the Post.*"*

"I didn't know the Post *had a voting guide."*

"Sure, it's perfect for you." Jane smiled. "It's in comic strip format."

The day for voting arrives, and the event receives wide media attention.

"The Electronic Congress is now in session," the TV news reader announces. "Touch-Tone telephone signals are proclaiming the will of the American people in a democratic ritual never envisioned by our founding fathers. Now entering its sixth year, the Electronic Congress has become an integral part of national political life."

Jane spread her newspaper voting guide on her desk and dialed "1-800-111-1134." A computerized voice answered her call.

"Hello, this is the Electronic Congress Voting System. Please enter your identification number now. If you make a mistake, please press the pound [#] symbol and try again."

Jane entered "1-6-2-3-8-9-1-7-9-0-7-4-6."

"Thank you. Your last name is spelled R-O-S-S. If that is correct, please press the star [*] symbol to continue. If that is wrong, please press the pound symbol and try again."

"*."

"Thank you. Question One is a binding vote on House Resolution 122 which will close 31 military bases in the United States. If your response is yes, for approval, please press 1. If your response is no, against approval, please press 2. If you wish to abstain on this issue, please press 0."

Jane glanced down at her newspaper to check which choice she had circled in her voting guide, then pressed "1."

"1, yes. If that is correct, please press the star symbol to continue. If that is wrong, please press the pound symbol and vote again."

"*."

"Thank you. Question Two is a binding vote on House Resolution 2039 which will increase federal funding for the ..."

Jane pressed "2" for disapproval before the voice finished.

"2, no. If that is correct, please..."

Jane interrupted again by pressing the star symbol to move on.

"If you wish to vote on the advisory questions, please press 1 for yes. If not, please press 2 for no."

"1, yes. If that is correct, please press the star symbol to continue. If that is wrong, please press the pound symbol and select your choice again."

".*"*

"Thank you. Advisory Question One is a non-binding vote on tax credits for urban enterprise zones. Please respond to Advisory Question One by pressing a number at any time. Please enter the number which corresponds to your choice in the voting guide. If you wish to abstain on this advisory question, please press 0."

Jane looked at her voting guide under Advisory Question One. Choice 1 was "No, tax credits should not be offered for urban enterprise zones." Choice 2 was "Yes, tax credits should be offered for urban enterprise zones for both new and existing investments." Choice 3 was "Yes, tax credits should be offered for urban enterprise zones for new investments only." Jane recognized that as her preference and pressed "3."

When Jane completed voting on the advisory questions she pressed the star symbol to confirm her last choice.

The voice responded, "You have now completed voting. Thank you."

A day later news media announced the results:

"According to the Federal Election Commission,

*58 percent of the electorate participated in the March
Electronic Congress. Voters supported House Resolution 122 with an unexpected 54 percent popular
vote. In the House of Representatives the actual vote
on the bill, which closes 31 military bases, was 341
votes in favor, with 94 against. The Senate vote was
by a more lopsided margin, with only seven states
casting 14 votes against the base closings. Pollsters
attribute the surprising result to a shift in the undecided voters in the last few days."*

"On House Resolution 2039..."

*The silence was deafening. Charlie Williams
could not believe the news. In the last few days of the
campaign against House Resolution 122 he had
convinced himself of victory. His pollsters claimed a
break-even vote two days before the referendum. No
one in the room spoke. Williams got up and left the
room. Ed finally broke the silence.*

*"I can't believe it. We realized we could lose, but
not like this. We were sure it would be a cliff-hanger."*

"What do you think happened?"

*"Damned if I know. I'll ask Charlie for his
assessment. He'll be back in a few minutes, but don't
expect any profound explanations. He was not ex-
pecting this. Not at all."*

*Senator Lupo smiled as Senator Quinn and both
their staff members gathered in her office. Quinn
shook her hand and beamed back. Lupo turned to
Roger Goldberg.*

"Roger, why don't you present the results and your recommendations for our next move?"

"Gladly."

Roger Goldberg handed out copies of the graph he had prepared for the meeting.

"We had very favorable results on all three variations of the bill, although the third version got the most votes. The follow-up question was the most significant: 'Would you support the other versions of this bill if put to a binding vote?' Over 80 percent said, 'yes.' That's solid support."

"Do we have to bother with a referendum?" asked Quinn.

"Personally, I don't think so. With the support and publicity we got for urban enterprise zones in this referendum, I think we can expect smooth sailing. I propose that we contact our friends in the House and start rounding up sponsors for bills in both houses."

"I agree, Roger."

"Any objections?" Quinn looked around the room. "Then let's go for it."

On the Wednesday after the March referendum the television set above the bar in a neighborhood tavern showed the President of the United States signing the bills approved by the American public in the recent referendum.

"Did you vote this weekend, Willy?" asked a young man.

"I sure did. And my bill came in a winner."

"What do you mean by 'came in a winner?' It's not a horse, Willy."

"Yeah, I know. But I feel like I picked a winner at the races."

"Well, why don't you buy me a drink with your winnings?"

"Don't be a wise guy," Willy laughed.

"I still don't trust politicians," remarked the young man.

"Then why do you still let them decide everything for you?"

The young man did not answer.

A New Synthesis

Somewhere between the proud, hopeful America of my youth and the cynical, doubtful America of today, we have lost our way. We have made some wrong turns and now find ourselves in the midst of a national crisis. We distrust our elected leaders, our politicians and our political parties. In most elections a majority of Americans do not even bother to vote. We feel isolated from our own government and feel powerless to do anything about it.

I have proposed the Electronic Congress to help restore people's faith in government. The concept is a moderate approach to direct democracy that is intended, not to supplant Congress, but to support it. National referendums will return many Americans to the political process. Betty H. Zisk, after her seven-year study of state-ballot questions, concluded that "while these mechanisms for direct democracy are hardly the universal panacea that some past reformers have claimed, they have helped to open up new pathways for participation, for political communication and even for policy innovation. This is no mean accomplishment for a simple set of procedural devices!"[1]

The ideas underlying the Electronic Congress are not mine, nor are they new. The late Buckminster Fuller told the U.S. Senate in 1975, "I proposed...voting by telephone on all prominent questions before Congress. That was back in 1940. It allows for continuous correction of the course...without political scapegoating. Today democracy is not working.... Particularly among the young there is a feeling of absolute futility."[2]

George Gallup Sr., after more than 50 years in the polling business, said, "On most major issues we've dealt with in the past 50 years, the public was more likely to be right—based on the judgment of history—than the legislatures or Congress."[3] Three years later, in a 1987 Gallup poll of American attitudes on direct democracy, an overwhelming 76 percent of the respondents indicated that they did not "trust our elected officials to make public decisions on all issues" but felt that "the voters should have a direct say on some issues."[4]

As one of those voters, I, too, want a direct say on issues. I am tired of feeling powerless. I am no longer satisfied with voting for candidates and hoping they will vote for legislation that I support.

If we voted on binding ballot questions in the Electronic Congress, we would become part of the legislative process. If we proposed or voted on advisory questions, we would directly influence our representatives. Given this opportunity to make a difference, many more Americans would become involved in national affairs.

I have heard many people shrug off their ignorance of national affairs with the attitude: "I can't do anything about it. What difference does it make?" I find that my own interest in government sometimes lapses when I question whether investing so much time in staying informed is really worthwhile. With an Electronic Congress, we *could* make a difference.

Government would be more accountable to us, because we would be paying more attention. Although any law we passed would still be subject to presidential veto, such an action would not go unobserved, as happens so often now. A desperately needed campaign-finance reform law was recently passed by Congress, only to be quietly vetoed by President Bush. Had that law been approved in a national referendum, the public's awareness would have spotlighted his decision, making a veto most unlikely. Popular legislation, such as the Brady gun control bill, would not be stymied by special interests if the voting public were more aware.

The referendum process would make legislative decisions more public, partly because we would be making some of the decisions ourselves. Even those laws decided by our congressmen would be more familiar to us, because before voting on advisory questions we would learn more about the many bills they were considering. Our heightened awareness would increase the likelihood that the law would reflect the public will.

Advisory questions could be placed on the ballot through initiative petition. Using popular initiative, the public could put new items on the political agenda, making available fresh and creative ideas.

My greatest hope for the Electronic Congress is that it would allay cynicism and alienation. Now large donations to political campaigns, in essence, buy votes in Congress. We live with a system that has lost sight of its origins and its ideals. We must act on our dissatisfaction.

Our Declaration of Independence says that governments derive "their just Powers from the Consent of the Governed. That, whenever any form of Government becomes destructive of these ends, it is the Right of the People to alter or abolish it, and to institute new Government." We must modify our government to meet the needs of today. We have done it before and we can do it again.

For those readers who want to help bring the Electronic Congress to fruition or learn more about it, I have initiated the Electronic Congress Telephone Referendum Project, described in the Addendum. The Telephone Referendum Project is a working prototype that allows participants to vote in a mock Electronic Congress. Participation of a substantial number of voters in the Telephone Referendum Project could help persuade our legislators to adopt the Electronic Congress.

The American republic has been evolving since its invention by a group of citizens in the summer of 1787. It is a 200-year-old experiment that has always adapted to new situations. The Electronic Congress would be another such an adaptation. Merging referendum with our existing federal system of checks and balances, the Electronic Congress would create a new synthesis of traditional political structures. The Electronic Congress, empowering us as citizens, would represent another important step in the democratic evolution of our country.

Addendum

To encourage the development of the Electronic Congress I have established a Telephone Referendum Project which uses available technology to allow participants to vote by telephone on ballot questions concerning national issues.

The Electronic Congress Telephone Referendum Project is sponsored by an educational, non-profit organization and does not engage in partisan political activity. The project goals include refining all aspects of telephone referendums—the use of telephone and computer equipment, the wording and structure of ballot questions and the format of voting guides—so that telephone voting becomes easy and reliable.

The project does not depend on government or

philanthropic grants, but operates through modest fees charged to participants. An initial fee pays for registering each voter. Thereafter, each participant votes by calling a 900-number on the designated days. A small fee, which pays for long-distance charges and the costs of operating the project, is automatically billed to the caller through the caller's local telephone company. A participant can refrain from voting at any time and can resume voting at any time. A participant's expenses will depend on the number of times he or she votes in the Electronic Congress. There is no minimum number of referendums required of participants.

A participant in the project may be of any age. Students may be registered at a special rate by their teachers. The Telephone Referendum Project can heighten student interest in the study of topics related to ballot questions which often are based on actual House and Senate bills or participant initiatives.

Participants will receive voting guides before each Electronic Congress referendum which list and explain the ballot questions. The guides will also include instructions for voting with Touch-Tone telephones.

A board of advisors directs the selection of referendum questions, choosing from House and Senate bills which are timely and important to voters. Some ballot questions are initiatives from participants. If legislators are interested in posing advisory questions for an upcoming referendum, the board of advisors considers their requests.

The Electronic Congress votes are tallied by Congressional district and by state. The vote will reflect the ayes and nays in the House and Senate, as if binding legislation were actually being approved or disapproved by the voters. Overall popular vote will also be recorded for informational purposes.

Although the Electronic Congress is a federal electronic referendum system, the Telephone Referendum Project is available to assist local or state governments planning to establish electronic referendums by providing technical consultation on equipment, software, ballot questions, voting guides and costs.

The willingness of people to fund and participate in this experimental system of electronic democracy will help legitimize the Electronic Congress concept and create the momentum necessary to bring it to fruition. Our growing numbers will become a mandate for electronic referendums. The reader is invited to join in the Electronic Congress Telephone Referendum Project, to practice telephone voting on ballot questions and to help advance the concept as a workable reality.

The Electronic Congress
Telephone Referendum Project
REGISTRATION FORM

Please copy this form to enroll in the Electronic Congress.
PLEASE PRINT CLEARLY. You will be sent a voter
identification number and instructions. Thank you.

NAME ———————————————————————

STREET ADDRESS ———————————————

———————————————————————————

CITY ————————————————————————

STATE ———————————————————————

ZIP CODE ————————————————————

Social Security No. (optional) ————————————

U.S. Congressional District Number———— and/or
Name of U.S. Congressional Representative:

———————————————————————————

If you do not know your district number or the name of your
U.S. Congressman, call your county Board of Elections or
your local newspaper for help. If not, we will try to place
your vote in the correct district based on your address.

Please mail with a check or money order for $5 to:

> Electronic Congress Telephone Referendum Project
> P.O. Box 500
> Pipersville, PA 18947.

(The $5 fee defrays the cost of this
non-profit educational project.)

Notes

Chapter 1: An Era of Disillusionment

[1]Richard Lacayo, "Under Fire," *Time*, Vol. 135, No. 5 (January 29, 1991), p. 16.

[2]Charles E. Lindblom, *The Policy-Making Process* (Englewood Cliffs, New Jersey, 1980), p. 106.

[3]Stanley W. Cloud and Nancy Travel, "Mr. Smith Leaves Washington," *Time*, Vol. 139, No. 23 (June 8, 1992), p. 65.

[4]David Ellis, "Nobody Here but Us Chickens," *Time*, Vol. 139, No. 12 (March 23, 1992), p. 30.

[5]Nancy Travel, "Why Washington Doesn't Work," *Time*, Vol. 139, No. 14 (April 6, 1992), p. 20.

[6]*Statistical Abstracts of the United States*, Department of Commerce, (Washington, 1991), p. 270.

[7]Ibid., p. 268.

[8]William Greider, *Who Will Tell the People: The Betrayal of*

American Democracy, (New York, 1992), p. 23.

[9]Cloud and Travel, p. 64.

Chapter 2: Citizen Lawmakers

[1]*Time,* April 6, 1992, "Plutocratic Populist," p. 19.

[2]John Woestendick "Report from Boulder, Colo.," *The Philadelphia Inquirer,* January 27, 1991, p. 27.

[3]Brochure from Voting by Phone Foundation, 1630 30th Street, Suite A-307, Colorado 80301.

Chapter 3: An Evolving Democracy

[1]Alexander Hamilton, James Madison and John Jay, *The Federalist Papers* (1787-1788) ed. Garry Wills (New York, 1982), p. 42.

[2]Ibid., p. 44-46.

[3]Ibid., introduction by Garry Wills, p. xxii.

[4]Ibid., pp. 47-48.

[5]Ibid., p. 281.

[6]Ibid., p. 44.

[7]David D. Schmidt, *Citizen Lawmakers: The Ballot Initiative Revolution,* (Philadelphia, 1989), p 8.

[8]Ibid., pp. 8-9.

[9]Ibid., pp. 12-14.

[10]Thomas E. Cronin, *Direct Democracy: The Politics of Initiative, Referendum, and Recall,* (Cambridge, Massachusetts, 1989), pp. 165-171.

[11]U.S. Congress, Senate, Committee on the Judiciary, Subcommittee on the Constitution, *Voter Initiative Constitutional Amendment Hearings,* 95th Congress, First Session. (Washington, 1978), pp. 1-151.

[12]Ibid., p. 646.

[13]Schmidt, p. 177.

[14]David B. Magleby, *Direct Legislation: Voting on Ballot Propositions in the United States*, (Baltimore, 1984), p. 7.

[15]Cronin, p. 177.

[16]Ibid., pp. 177-179.

[17]Michael Kelly, "Perot's Vision: Consensus by Computer," *The New York Times*, January 6, 1992, p. 1 and 8.

[18]Hamilton, et al, (Madison), p. 45.

[19]Ibid.

[20]*Statistical Abstracts of the United States*, Department of Commerce. (Washington, 1991), p. 262.

[21]*Statistical Abstracts of the United States*, Department of Commerce (Washington, 1989), p. 273.

[22]Fred Wertheimer, "CC Heads Towards 20th Anniversary," *Common Cause Magazine* (November/December, 1989), p. 30.

[23]*Statistical Abstracts of the United States*, Department of Commerce (Washington, 1989), p. 544.

[24]Hamilton, et al, (Madison), p. 48.

[25]Christopher Cornell, "Perot's proposal for an 'electronic town meeting' would clog the lines," *The Philadelphia Inquirer*, June 9, 1992, p. A23.

[26]William Greider, *Who Will Tell the People: The Betrayal of American Democracy* (New York, 1992), p. 406.

Chapter 4: A Short History of Referendums

[1]David Butler and Austin Ranney, eds., *Referendums: A Comparative Study of Practice and Theory.* (Washington, 1978), p. 18.

[2]Ibid., pp. 123-128.

[3]Ibid., p.18.

[4]Ibid.

[5]Ibid., pp. 3-5.

[6]Ibid., pp. 10-14.

[7]Ibid.

[8]Ibid., p. 23.

[9]Ibid., p. 6.

[10]Ibid., pp. 39-40.

[11]Ibid., pp. 41-42.

[12]Thomas E. Cronin, *Direct Democracy: The Politics of Initiative, Referendum, and Recall,* (Cambridge, Massachusetts, 1989), p. 161.

[13]Butler and Ranney, pp. 50-64.

[14]Ibid., pp. 45-46.

[15]David D. Schmidt, *Citizen Lawmakers: The Ballot Initiative Revolution,* (Philadelphia, 1989), pp. 6-7.

[16]Cronin, p. 41.

[17]Butler and Ranney, pp. 69-74.

[18]Ibid., pp. 73-75.

[19]Ibid., pp. 76-77.

[20]Ibid., p. 78.

[21]Schmidt, pp. 15-19.

[22]Butler and Ranney, p. 79.

[23]Ibid., pp. 78-80.

[24]Ibid., pp. 80-81.

[25]Schmidt, pp. 20-24 and vii.

[26]Butler and Ranney, p. 80. The data for referendums proposed by legislators comes from only 18 states.

[27]Ibid., p. 84.

[28]Schmidt, p.37.

[29]The Bucks County referendum on the pumping station at Point

Pleasant was held on May 17, 1983. With a 52 percent turnout of eligible voters, Bucks County citizens voted to "Dump the Pump" by a 56 percent majority. (The *Daily Intelligencer*, May 19, 1983, p. 1). The pump was eventually built anyway because the courts upheld claims that the contracts had already been signed and that the county commissioners, who had followed the dictates of the advisory referendum, did not have the authority to stop the construction of the pump and related water systems.

[30]Michael Kelly, "Perot's Vision: Consensus by Computer," *The New York Times*, January 6, 1992, p. 8.

[31]Cronin, p. 220-221.

[32]A letter to the *New York Times*, June 21, 1992, from Jeffrey Abramson, co-author of *The Electronic Commonwealth: New Media Tecnhologies and Democratic Values* and professor of politics at Brandeis University.

[33]Ibid.

[34]Ibid.

[35]Philip Elmer-Dewitt, "Dial D for Democracy," *Time*, Vol. 139, No. 23 (June 8, 1992), p. 44.

Chapter 5: Assessing Voter Competence

[1]Harold F. Gosnell, *Democracy: The Threshold of Freedom* (New York, 1949), p. 258.

[2]Betty H. Zisk, *Money, Media and the Grass Roots: State Ballot Issues and the Electoral Process*, (Newbury Park, California, 1987), p. 192.

[3]Thomas E. Cronin, *Direct Democracy: The Politics of Initiative, Referendum, and Recall*, (Cambridge, Massachusetts, 1989), pp. 72-73.

[4]David D. Schmidt, *Citizen Lawmakers: The Ballot Initiative*

Revolution, (Philadelphia, 1989), pp. 125-145. Most of my information on Proposition 13 comes from Chapter 6: Tax Revolt.
[5]A paper by James A. Meader as quoted in Cronin, p. 72.
[6]Schmidt, p. 39.
[7]As quoted in Cronin, p. 48.
[8]Ibid., p. 66-67.
[9]David B. Magleby, *Direct Legislation: Voting on Ballot Propositions in the United States,* (Baltimore, 1984), p. 183.
[10]Cronin, p. 74.
[11]David Butler and Austin Ranney, eds., *Referendums: A Comparative Study of Practice and Theory.* (Washington, 1978), p. 112.
[12]Magleby, pp. 138-139.
[13]Ibid., p. 124.
[14]Zisk, p. 245.
[15]Cronin, pp. 109-111.
[16]Schmidt, p. 35.
[17]Cronin, p. 104.
[18]Ibid., p. 107.
[19]Schmidt as quoted in Cronin, p. 101.
[20]Cronin, p. 92-96.
[21]U.S. Congress, Senate, Committee on the Judiciary, Subcommittee on the Constitution, *Voter Initiative Constitutional Amendment Hearings,* 95th Congress, First Session. (Washington, D.C., 1978), p. 26.
[22]Stanley W. Cloud and Nancy Travel, "Mr. Smith Leaves Washington," *Time,* Vol. 139, No. 23 (June 8, 1992), p. 64.
[23]Schmidt, pp. 31-33.
[24]From an article by Tom Sherwood and Sandra Sugawara, "Committee Kills Bills by the Dozen: Richmond's Night of the

Long Knives, *"Washington Post* (February 7, 1983) as quoted in Schmidt, p. 33.

[25]William Greider, *Who Will Tell the People: The Betrayal of American Democracy* (New York, 1992), p. 16.
[26]Schmidt, p. 32.

Chapter 6: Telephone-Voting Technology
[1]John Woestendick, "Report from Boulder, Colo.," *The Philadelphia Inquirer,* January 27, 1991, p. 27.
[2]Ibid.
[3]Ibid.
[4]Presented on television program, "FBI Is Pushing for Greater Wiretapping Capabilities," ABC News *Nightline* (May 22, 1992).
[5]Christopher Cornell, "Perot's proposal for an 'electronic town meeting' would clog the lines," *The Philadelphia Inquirer,* June 9, 1992, p. A23.
[6]Telephone interviews with Rick Sachs and Mike McCarthy at Interactive Communication Systems, Inc., Colorado Springs, Colorado (April 20, June 4 and August 19, 1992).
[7]Telephone interviews with Rich Quintanilla at Interactive Information Systems, Denver, Colorado (April 20 and June 4, 1992).
[8]Louis Jacobson, "Let Your Fingers Do the Voting, Maybe," *The Wall Street Journal,* August 12, 1992, p. B1.

Chapter 8: A New Synthesis
[1]Betty H. Zisk, *Money, Media and the Grass Roots: State Ballot Issues and the Electoral Process,* (Newbury Park, Califorinia, 1987), p. 248.

²Brochure from Voting by Phone Foundation, 1630 30th Street, Suite A-307, Colorado 80301.

³David D. Schmidt, *Citizen Lawmakers: The Ballot Initiative Revolution,* (Philadelphia, 1989), p. 40.

⁴Thomas E. Cronin, *Direct Democracy: The Politics of Initiative, Referendum, and Recall,* (Cambridge, Massachusetts, 1989), p. 80.

Selected Bibliography

Readers who want to learn more about initiative and referendum will appreciate the following books by contemporary political scientists. I am indebted to them for providing much of the information I needed to write *The Electronic Congress*.

Butler, David and Austin Ranney, eds. *Referendums: A Comparative Study of Practice and Theory*. Washington, D.C.: American Enterprise Institute for Public Policy Research, 1978.

Cronin, Thomas E. *Direct Democracy: The Politics of Initiative, Referendum, and Recall*. Cambridge, Massachusetts: Harvard University Press, 1989.

Magleby, David B. *Direct Legislation: Voting on Ballot Propositions in the United States.* Baltimore: The Johns Hopkins University Press, 1984.

Schmidt, David D. *Citizen Lawmakers: The Ballot Initiative Revolution.* Philadelphia, Pennsylvania: Temple University Press, 1989.

Betty H. Zisk, *Money, Media, and the Grass Roots: State Ballot Issues and the Electoral Process.* Newbury Park, California: Sage Publications, 1987.

Index

Telephones, percentage of
households with, 38, 80
Telephone Referendum Project,
104-105, 107-109, 111
Telephone voting, 14-15, 19, 21
55, 57, 74-82, 95-97, 102,
107-109; Liberal Party in
Nova Scotia, 82; Gulf War
soldiers by fax, 82
Televisions, percentage of
households with, 38
Televoting, 55
Texas, 32
Thomas, Clarence, 39
Thompson, Ken, 69
TOUGHLOVE, 7

Veto, presidential, 16, 18, 103
Vietnam War, 3, 5
Virginia, 33, 70-71
Voter registration, 77-78, 81
Voter turnout in elections, 10-11,
77; African-Americans, 11
Voting by Phone Foundation, 14,
75, 76
Voting guides, 15, 32, 64,76, 94-
95, 97, 107, 108
Voting machines, 74, 78, 81-82

War referendum, 29-30
Watergate, 4,5

Weber, Vin, 9
Wyoming, 16, 29, 31

Zisk, Betty H., 59-60, 65, 101-
102

Acknowledgements

I wrote *The Electronic Congress* while meeting the demands of my full-time job as director of the Community Service Foundation. My wife Susan, who has her own full-time job in the same organization, graciously assumed or assisted me with many of my household and other responsibilities. She also read the manuscript as it progressed and gave me honest feedback, which was sometimes difficult because she was not always telling me what I wanted to hear.

I employed my elder son Joshua, a college history major, during his vacation to do research and editing. His energy and enthusiasm buoyed me and moved the book toward completion.

My younger son Ben, Mitch Bunkin and Dan

Sullivan read the first draft and provided me with much needed encouragment.

Alexei and Cory Panshin did editing work on the first draft and provided me with much needed criticism that pushed me to largely rewrite the entire manuscript. I thank them for their candor.

John Koch steered me to Nancy Lockwood, an editor whose thorough and intelligent editing was vital to the final manuscript.

Evan Ravitz, director of the Voting by Phone Foundation, guided me to companies working with computer programs and equipment for telephone voting. Rick Sachs and Mike McCarthy at Interactive Communication Systems answered my many questions.

Illustrator and designer Ed Piechocki generously supported my efforts by translating the idea of *The Electronic Congress* into an outstanding cover design, as well as producing the logo and letterhead for The Piper's Press.

Bill Sabatino gave me ongoing commentary on the manuscript and a steady stream of relevant articles, editorials and letters to the editor from various newspapers. His faith in my idea is one of the primary reasons I brought it to fruition.

My parents, Phyllis and Morris Wachtel, helped me with some final proofreading.

Thank you all.

—Ted Wachtel, August 23, 1992

To order copies of
The Electronic Congress
please copy the form below and send
with a check or money order
for $12.95
for each copy to:

The Piper's Press
P.O. Box 400
Pipersville, PA 18947

Name _____

Address _____

City _____ State ___ Zip Code _____

Quantity of books_____ X $12.95= _____
plus 6% sales (in Penna. only) _____
TOTAL _____